STORIES IN HISTORY

ANCIENT ROME

200 B.C. – A.D. 350

Cover illustration: Todd Leonardo

Printed in the United States of America
ISBN 0-618-14212-6

3 4 5 6 7 — DCI — 06 05 04 03 02

Table of Contents

PART I: THE REPUBLIC

*When Benny reaches for the computer mouse, a
strange thing happens. Hannibal, Rome's lifelong
enemy, is going to launch a surprise attack. With
an army of infantry, cavalry, and war elephants,
he will march across the snowy Alps. The Roman
Republic is now in the Second Punic War.*

PART II: THE EMPIRE

About this Book

The stories are historical fiction. They are based on historical fact, but some of the characters and events may be fictional. In the Sources section you'll learn which is which and where the information came from.

The illustrations are all historical. If they are from a time different from the story, the caption tells you. Original documents help you understand the time period. Maps let you know where things were.

Items explained in People and Terms to Know are repeated in the Glossary. Look there if you come across a name or term you don't know.

Historians do not always agree on the exact dates of events in the ancient past. The letter c before a date, means "about" (from the Latin word circa).

If you would like to read more about these exciting times, you will find recommendations in Reading on Your Own.

This 19th-century engraving shows Roman soldiers battling Spartacus and his rebel gladiators. ▶

Background

*Lions do not fight with one another, serpents
do not attack serpents, nor do wild monsters
of the deep rage against their kind. But most of the
calamities of man are caused by his fellow man.*

—Pliny the Elder,
Natural History

Rome's Beginnings

Today's Roman citizens can stand on one of their city's seven hills and look out over statues and buildings made two thousand years ago. But Rome is even older than that. According to legend, the city was founded in 753 B.C. by one of two twin boys. As babies, Romulus and Remus were put in a basket and tossed into the Tiber River. Rescued by a she-wolf who nursed them, the twins lived and grew up. One of them, Romulus, founded Rome on a hill near the Tiber and became Rome's first king. After that, Rome supposedly had seven kings. The last of them were Etruscans, people from cities in northern and central Italy. The Romans defeated the last Etruscan king in about 509 B.C., and Rome became a republic that lasted for nearly 500 years.

▲
When the Romans founded a new town, they held a sacred ceremony. A line made with an ox-drawn plow marked the town's boundaries.

The Roman Republic

"The gods are on the side of the stronger."

—Tacitus, *Histories*

A republic is a state in which the power rests with the citizens. The government is run by people the citizens elect. There is no king or queen. In the Roman Republic, however, the citizens were not all equal.

Until about the third century B.C., men from the upper classes, the *patricians* (puh•TRISH•uhnz), ran the government. You were a patrician if you had money, owned land, or came from a respected family.

There were three parts to the government of the republic: (1) The magistrates, or top government officials (see the chart on the next page), (2) the senate, and (3) the people. Only adult patrician men were part of the government. Women, slaves, and foreigners had no part in government affairs.

During the first 200 or so years of the republic, there was much unrest. In Rome, the *plebeians* (plih•BEE•uhnz), or common people, continually protested for fairer treatment and a bigger voice in the government. Outside Rome there were Roman colonies in the north, east, and south of Italy. Many of the people in these colonies were very different from the Romans. They were different in customs and language, and were often unfriendly. In an effort to keep peace, the Romans gave some of these colonies Roman citizenship. It was usually considered a prize. Other colonies had no rights in Rome, nor did they wish them.

Magistrates

consul—either of the two chief magistrates, chosen every year, who served one year. He might lead an army, propose laws, call the senate together, and conduct other state business.

dictator—appointed to lead only in times of emergency or crisis. Traditionally, he could serve up to six months only.

censor—one of two officials in charge of taking the public census and looking after public morals. He was also awarded government contracts for building bridges and roads.

praetor (PREE•tuhr)—annually elected official in charge of the courts and having many of the same duties as a consul.

quaestor (KWES•tuhr)—official responsible for finance and the treasury.

aedile (EE•dyl)—official responsible for public works and games and who supervised markets, the grain supply, and the water supply.

tribunes—officers elected by the adult male common people (plebeians) to protect their rights.

senate—The number of senators varied throughout the years, but there were usually 300. The senate advised the various magistrates. Senators were not elected but were recommended for office by a consul. They could not pass laws, but they were powerful. Senators usually held office for life.

The Punic Wars

"Carthage must be destroyed."

—Cato the Elder,
speech to the Roman Senate

Carthage (KAI IR•thihj) in North Africa was a Phoenician (fih•NEE•shuhn) city-state. *Punica* was the Latin word for "Phoenician," so Rome's three wars with these people are known as the Punic Wars. By the end of these wars, Rome controlled an empire.

The Phoenicians had long been known for their excellent sailing ships. Carthage especially had a fine fleet. The First Punic War began on the island of Sicily, which lies just off the southwest coast of Italy. (See the map on page 14.) Carthage controlled half the island. Rome feared the Carthaginians would try to use Sicily as a base to invade Italy. So the Romans built a navy. In battle after battle, they lost to Carthage. Finally they won. Sicily became the first Roman colony outside Italy.

The Second Punic War started twenty years later. The Carthaginian general Hannibal wanted revenge. He marched his troops from Spain across the Alps, the mountains that form the northern border of Italy. He surprised the Romans and defeated them in several battles. But the Romans recovered and finally won the war. In the third and last Punic War, Carthage was again defeated. By this time, Rome had won Spain from Carthage and had conquered parts of Gaul (now France) and much of the eastern Mediterranean.

The Rise and Fall of Caesar

"I came, I saw, I conquered."

—Julius Caesar,
describing one of his military campaigns

What lay ahead for Rome to conquer? Asia Minor, Syria, Palestine, Egypt, North Africa, the rest of Gaul, and Britain would be added to the Empire. Rome and its armies seemed determined to take over much of the world.

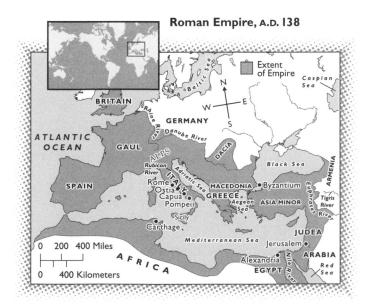

Roman Empire, A.D. 138

Several powerful Roman commanders rose in the first century B.C. Each had his own army. The result was a series of civil wars. In the end, Julius Caesar (SEE•zuhr) defeated his major rivals.

Caesar was a brilliant general and politician. He conquered Gaul between 58 and 51 B.C. This made him a hero to the Roman people. In Rome, the general Pompey was consul. He and the senate feared Caesar. When Caesar proposed to take his army back to Rome, Pompey and the senate ordered him not to. Nevertheless, Caesar crossed the Rubicon River into Italy, and this started a civil war. Caesar defeated Pompey a year later. Now that he was such a hero, the senate made him dictator for life. He was popular with many citizens and started many reforms.

▲
This Roman silver coin was produced to honor the men who killed Caesar. Brutus is on one side. On the other side, two daggers lie on either side of the "Liberty cap" given to a freed slave.

Yet some feared that he would end the republic by becoming king. As a result, a group of senators led by Cassius and Brutus stabbed him to death in 44 B.C.

The Empire

*"After this time I surpassed all others in authority,
but I had no more power than the others who were also
my colleagues in office."*

—Augustus Caesar,
on the history of his reign

Fearing death from angry mobs, Brutus and
Cassius fled Rome. They were pursued by Caesar's
friend Mark Antony and his adopted son Octavian.
Antony and Octavian's armies beat them in a battle
in Greece in 42 B.C. Both Brutus and Cassius died.
Now Antony and Octavian, with a consul named
Lepidus, formed a triumvirate (try•UHM•vuhr•iht),
a government of three, to rule the empire. Lepidus
was soon unseated. Then Antony and Octavian
became rivals for power.

Antony joined forces with Cleopatra, the
queen of Egypt. He hoped to build a strong base
of power in the eastern Mediterranean. Fearing
Cleopatra's influence and backed by Rome,
Octavian defeated Antony in a naval battle at
Actium in Greece in 31 B.C. The way was clear for
Octavian to take complete control.

Octavian became an emperor. The Romans were
tired of war. Few seemed to care that the government

was now ruled by one man alone. Octavian's name was changed to Augustus ("honored one"), and he changed the face of Rome. Although the senate still had some powers, Augustus was a strong leader. The long years of the *Pax Romana* ("Roman peace") that followed, though not always trouble-free, made sure that his rule would stand as a symbol of Rome's greatness.

Augustus died in A.D. 14. In the following years, a series of emperors, some good, some terrible, followed. Tiberius, Caligula, Claudius, Nero, Hadrian, and Marcus Aurelius are only some of the rulers whose stories make up Roman history.

Barbarian prisoners are brought before the Roman emperor Marcus Aurelius during the wars against the Germanic tribes. ▶

In A.D. 286, the emperor Diocletian divided the empire into eastern and western halves. Each half had two rulers. Constantine, who had been an army officer, beat his western co-ruler in a battle in 312. That made him the only emperor of the Western Empire.

Constantine defeated the eastern emperor in 323. He chose the city of Byzantium as his capital. The city was located on the narrow waterway that divided the Black Sea from the Mediterranean Sea, at the crossroads between Europe and Asia. (See the map on page 14.) He renamed it Constantinople (now Istanbul), and it became a dazzling city. Constantine was then the sole ruler of the entire Roman Empire.

In 324, Constantine made world history by becoming the first Christian emperor. His conversion meant an end to the ill-treatment of Christians at the hands of the Romans.

In the following century, the Western Empire would be overrun by migrating tribes from the north and east. But the Roman Empire survived in the east until 1453, when it finally fell to the Ottoman Turks.

Daily Life in Ancient Rome

"This is what I had prayed for: a small piece of land
With a garden, a fresh-flowing spring of water at hand
Near the house, and, above and behind, a small forest stand."

—Horace

Like many Romans, the poet Horace wanted to get away from the city. In another poem, he wrote of the "smoke, and the grandeur and the noise" of Rome. The city must have had all of those things. Some people have estimated that early in the first century A.D. there were about a million people living there.

Some ordinary people lived in buildings that looked very much like today's small apartment houses. They bought bread from a baker's shop, bathed at public baths, and found entertainment at the theater or watching the gladiators' contests. They made a living by providing what people needed to eat, wear, and use in daily life.

Rich Romans, the patricians, sent servants to do the shopping and entertained guests with huge dinners at home. Guests might listen to music played on stringed instruments. Or they might hear someone recite poetry. The patricians spent time at their seaside villas and took an active part in government affairs in the city.

A Roman butcher works in his shop.

Life in Rome was far from perfect. Ambitious men and women were sometimes willing to cheat and murder to gain power. The wishes of the plebeians, many of them poor, were often ignored by officials who refused to grant them their rights.

Many of the people captured by Roman armies were taken to the city and pressed into slavery. Some were trained as gladiators to fight against other gladiators or against wild animals. In huge arenas, they often fought to a bloody death while an eager crowd looked on and cheered. Other slaves, both men and women, served in the households of wealthy Romans. Slaves could become free, however, and some freed slaves rented shops or even became land owners.

Reminders of Roman Life

M uch of what we know about Roman civilization comes from written records. These records include the writings of historians such as Tacitus and poets such as Horace. We also know about the way the Romans lived from the objects they made. These can be everyday objects such as sandals and pottery. They can also be beautiful works of art such as wall paintings and statues.

One of the most famous sources for our knowledge of Roman life is the city of Pompeii. The city was completely buried when a nearby volcano, Mount Vesuvius, erupted in A.D. 79. Pompeii had been long forgotten when it was found by accident in the middle of the 1700s. Since then, scholars have worked at uncovering the city. They have found the remains of streets, houses, shops, works of art, everyday objects, and even food.

All these things help us learn about Rome and its people. But even without them, reminders of Roman civilization are all around us. The letters of our alphabet, our calendar (including the names of several of the months), thousands of our words, our laws, our public buildings, and many other parts of our lives have been shaped by Roman civilization.

The cooking pots in this kitchen in Pompeii were left behind when the people of the house fled the eruption of Vesuvius in A.D. 79.

Time Line

753 B.C.—Rome is founded.

509 B.C.—Roman Republic is founded.

312 B.C.—The Appian Way is begun.

218–201 B.C.—Second Punic War.

149–146 B.C.—Third Punic War.

73–71 B.C.—Spartacus leads a slave revolt.

58–51 B.C.—Caesar conquers Gaul. Roman troops land in Britain.

44 B.C.—Caesar is murdered.

31 B.C.—Octavian defeats Antony and Cleopatra.

27 B.C.—Octavian becomes the first emperor, Augustus.

A.D. 41—Claudius becomes emperor.

A.D. 79—Mount Vesuvius erupts. Pompeii is buried.

A.D. 286—Emperor Diocletian divides the empire.

A.D. 306–337—Reign of Constantine, who establishes capital of Eastern Empire at Constantinople.

A.D. 476—Western Empire falls.

The Republic

chapter three

Hannibal Dot Com

BY STEPHEN CURRIE

"A whole report to write on Roman times," said Benny's best friend, James. He cleared some papers off the computer desk chair and sat down gloomily.

"Boring." Benny slumped on the couch. "What's so great about Rome, anyway? Falling-apart buildings and people wearing sheets."

"We could do someone who attacked Rome." James's eyes flew down the list they'd been given in school. "Maybe this guy **Hannibal**."

Whoever Hannibal was, thought Benny. "Boring," he said again. "I vote you get some books from the library." *Then you can read them and write the report*

People and Terms to Know

Hannibal (HAN•uh•buhl)—(247– 183 B.C.) general from Carthage, a city-state on the Mediterranean coast of Africa. Hannibal was Rome's enemy in the Second Punic War.

Hannibal's troops move their war elephants across a river on rafts. They are on the way to invade Italy. This painting was done nearly 1,600 years later.

while I play games on your computer, he added to himself.

James shook his head. "We have the Internet. Let's use the computer."

James logged onto the Internet and clicked a few keys. "We'll start with Hannibal, anyway," he said over his shoulder. A list of web pages scrolled onto the screen. "And if he's boring we'll try someone else, okay?"

Benny reached for the computer mouse. Why should James have all the fun? "How about we try this page?" He slid the mouse to the link and clicked—

The screen spun. The mouse seemed to break off in Benny's hand. And all at once, he wasn't in James's living room any more.

Instead, he was on a mountain, and he was freezing cold.

*   *   *

"Ah, another new soldier!"

Benny scrambled to his feet. In front of him stood a thin man with a sword who looked even colder than Benny. "What nation are you?" he asked.

"Um—" Benny realized that he was knee-deep in snow. "I'm an American."

"A new one for me." The man smiled. "We have soldiers of many nations, though. I'm from Carthage myself, but there are Spaniards, Numidians, Celts. . . . My name's Nico. I'm sure Hannibal will be pleased to see you."

Benny frowned as a trumpet sounded somewhere in the distance. "Hannibal?"

——————

What were elephants doing in the Alps? *he wondered.*

——————

"Our leader!" Nico clapped Benny on the shoulder.

Benny shivered. "Why are we—here?" *This sure is some web page,* he thought. He looked up at the steep cliffs surrounding him. He saw the endless rows of soldiers clambering through a snowy pass ahead. Like Nico, they all looked underfed. They were armed with little more than spears.

"Hannibal's launching a surprise attack against the Romans," Nico explained. "Unfortunately, the Alps were between us and them. So here we are, elephants and all."

Elephants! Remembering the trumpeting noise, Benny whirled and stared. Behind him several men were leading a protesting elephant down the slope. The elephant looked cold and terribly thin. *What were elephants doing in the Alps?* he wondered.

"Surprised?" said Nico. "They're wonderful animals for a war. You haven't lived till you've seen a whole line of forty elephants with their sharp tusks showing and running toward the other army ready to attack. They terrify the enemy's horses—and the enemy himself, of course—but I fear ours won't last much longer." He drew his thin cloak around him. "Already we've lost hundreds of good men, and they're better suited to the climate than the elephants are. Better keep moving, friend. It's cold."

Benny didn't have to be told twice. "Why cross in winter, though?" he asked, gingerly picking his way across the ice.

The soldier frowned. "Hannibal heard that the Romans were planning an attack of their own. If they fight, we fight. Alas, summer is over, so now we must deal with ice, snowslides, wind, cold, and hunger." He sneezed. "The timing was a dreadful mistake, friend."

Benny shaded his eyes and gazed into the distance. The men stumbled down the frozen path. All were as cold and hungry as Nico. Rocks fell from the cliffs, narrowly missing the soldiers. "You guys must really hate the Romans," he said.

Nico gave a humorless laugh. "Why, our army in Carthage has been fighting with Rome for forty years," he said. "There's been a war ever since my father was a boy. And it's always the same story—land! Those Romans barge in and take over everybody else's territory—Spain, Africa, you name it. Why, I bet they won't stop till they've conquered the whole world!" Nico's skinny fists, slightly blue from the cold, clenched and unclenched. "Even—America? That's the name of your country, isn't it?"

"Assuming they can find it," Benny murmured to himself. "That's right," he said aloud. He wished he had a pair of gloves.

"It's not even any good for the Romans, you know." Nico shuffled forward through a bank of drifted snow. "Fighting wars costs money, so they make everybody pay heavy taxes.

"Those Romans barge in and take over everybody else's territory— Spain, Africa, you name it."

The poor can scarcely manage to stay alive at all." He blew on his hands to warm them.

Benny lifted his hands to do the same. Then remembered that he was wearing jeans. Quickly he jammed his hands into his pockets for warmth.

"Not that I waste sympathy on the Romans when they keep grabbing land from everybody else," Nico began.

But Benny's hand had accidentally clicked the computer mouse in his pocket. Suddenly the mountains, the elephant, and Nico were gone.

* * *

"Victory!" a familiar voice shouted next to Benny's ear. "All hail to Hannibal!"

Benny opened one eye. He wasn't cold any more. In fact, he was downright hot in the summer sun. The mountains, too, had been replaced by a broad flat plain. Trees lined the horizon. It looked like pictures he had seen of Italy. Maybe, he thought with a sudden flash of excitement, he was close to Rome itself.

"My friend!" Benny turned as Nico clapped him on the back. Benny realized why the voice had sounded so familiar. "Remember me? I talked with you in the Alps a couple of years back!"

A couple of years! Benny swallowed hard. This war was certainly taking its time. "Sure, Nico. I remember. Good to see you again."

"What a victory, my friend!" Nico was bouncing with joy. "The plains of **Cannae** are ours! They had

---

People and Terms to Know

Cannae (KAN•ee)—village in southeastern Italy, where Hannibal defeated the Romans in 216 B.C. About 50,000 Romans were killed, compared to about 6,000 soldiers in Hannibal's army.

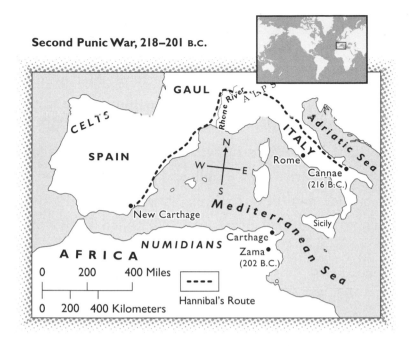

Second Punic War, 218–201 B.C.

Hannibal's Route

more soldiers, but we had an international army—and Hannibal had his great strategies." He laughed. "As I said, everybody hates the Romans. Even Americans like you!"

"Long live Hannibal, winner of the Battle of Cannae!" someone shouted.

"On to Rome!" Nico shouted again. "This war will soon be over, and the hated Romans will be defeated!" He pulled a handful of coins from a bag and tossed them high into the air. "Victory is ours! Throw your coins, friend!"

Benny dug into his pocket, forgetting what else was inside. When he looked up, the plains were gone and the cheering soldiers with them.

* * *

A desert stretched in all directions. Men were lined up on all sides of him. Benny thought he was probably standing somewhere on a North African battlefield. Perhaps he was not far from Carthage itself. He turned to his right and gasped.

The man next to him, standing straight as a spear, was Nico, but a much older Nico. He was a battle-worn Nico, now weaponless and choking back tears.

"It's been a while, my friend," Nico said. "A sad day to meet again. A sad place, too, here at **Zama**. I had such hopes. . . ." His voice trailed off.

Frowning, Benny stared past the rows of assembled soldiers. They looked old and weary like Nico. How many years had he fast-forwarded this time? Across the field he could see the Roman army. Thousands upon thousands of warriors stood with swords and shields. Between the armies, two bearded men were talking.

"I hope that Roman general **Scipio Africanus** offers Hannibal good terms of peace," said Nico. "But I will mourn this day forever; we have lost."

People and Terms to Know

Zama (ZAY•muh)—North African site of the final battle in the Second Punic War (202 B.C.). Rome won; Carthage lost.

Scipio Africanus (SIHP•ee•OH af•rih•KAHN•uhs)—(c. 236–183 B.C.) great Roman general who won the Battle of Zama. He let Hannibal return to Carthage but made Carthage become a Roman ally.

"Lost?" The news made Benny feel as if he'd been punched in the stomach.

"Not Hannibal's fault," Nico murmured. "They had too many soldiers, and there was no way into the city of Rome. We fought for sixteen years." He shook his head.

Sixteen years of fighting! Benny shut his eyes and tried to think of something comforting to say. "It was a hard fight," he told Nico. "And I bet they'll remember Hannibal and his army for years to come."

"Do you think so?" Nico brightened.

"I know so," said Benny, patting his thigh for emphasis. Again, he had forgotten what he had in his pocket.

* * *

"Aw, that web page doesn't want to load," said James, his voice full of disgust. "Hey, let's switch to another topic. You thought Hannibal was pretty boring anyway. How about. . . ."

Benny took a deep breath. *Actually, that page loaded just fine,* he thought. He took the mouse out of his pocket and hooked it back into place. His head whirled with questions. Why had Hannibal hated Rome so much? How had he managed to win the Battle of Cannae? How had his troops kept fighting for sixteen years? What were the peace terms?

And what had happened to the elephants?

"You know what?" Benny said. "I think I changed my mind. Let's do Hannibal, after all."

QUESTIONS TO CONSIDER

1. What advantages did Hannibal have in fighting the war against Rome? What advantages did the Romans have?

2. What does the story tell you about the power and popularity of the Roman Empire during this time?

3. How do you think the wars between Rome and Carthage affected life in the Roman Republic?

4. Why do you think Hannibal's story is better known today than that of the Roman general who defeated him?

The Gracchi and the Roman Republic

BY JUDITH LLOYD YERO

Rome's empire grew in the 2nd century B.C. Wealth poured into the city. One problem this new wealth created was a widening gap between rich and poor. Many of Rome's poor were farmers who had served as soldiers in Rome's wars of expansion. By Roman custom, only farmers who owned land could serve in the army. They had something to fight for. During Rome's wars, many of these farmer soldiers were away for years. While they were gone, wealthy Romans took over the soldiers' farms. The wealthy used slaves to work the land. When the soldiers returned, their farms were gone. These landless farmers and their families lived in Rome's slums and begged for food.

Cornelia identifies her children as her "jewels" in this painting by Philipp

Two Roman reformers who tried to do something about these problems were the brothers **Tiberius** and **Gaius Gracchus**. Known as "the Gracchi" (GRAK•eye), the brothers were the first of a series of political leaders who got their support from the common people of Rome. The Gracchi were members of Rome's ruling class. Their parents guided them from birth to be Roman leaders. The boys were given a fine education in Greek and Latin from private tutors. When Tiberius was ten and Gaius just a baby, their father died and their mother, Cornelia, took over the task of preparing her sons for greatness. Cornelia took great pride in her boys. Once, when a noble Roman lady showed off her fine ornaments, Cornelia pointed to her boys and said, "These are my jewels!" Cornelia has been a symbol of the ideal Roman mother ever since.

Tiberius showed great promise as a speaker and leader. While in the army, he saw how much land had been taken over by the wealthy. Where would

People and Terms to Know

Tiberius Gracchus (ty•BEER•ee•uhs GRAK•uhs)—(163–133 B.C.) elder son of Tiberius Gracchus, a Roman consul, and Cornelia, daughter of Scipio Africanus, the conqueror of Hannibal. Tiberius was known as a brave soldier and a calm, but powerful, speaker.

Gaius Gracchus (GY•uhs GRAK•uhs) (153–121 B.C.)—younger son of Tiberius Gracchus and Cornelia. Gaius was a more fiery speaker than his older brother.

the soldiers come from if farmers no longer worked the land? What would become of the farmers who could no longer support themselves and their families?

In 134 B.C., Tiberius was elected a **tribune** of the people. Rome was suffering from a shortage of grain. The farmers that had supplied grain no longer worked the land, and the wealthy landowners preferred to grow crops that made more profit, such as olives that could be pressed into oil.

Tiberius reminded the people of an old Roman law. It said that no one could hold more than about 300 acres of land. Because the law had never been enforced, the wealthy, including many Roman senators, often had thousands of acres.

Tiberius proposed a new law that said that those who held more than their legal share of land must give it up so that the land could be fairly distributed to the farmers. Farmers would pay rent on their new land, but were forbidden to sell it. This prevented them from selling the land back to the wealthy.

People and Terms to Know

tribune—representative elected by the people's assembly. There were ten tribunes, any one of whom could call the people's assembly together or forbid that a proposal come before the assembly.

The common people loved the idea, but the wealthy hated it. They had invested their own money in the crops and buildings on the land and saw their wealth threatened. Senators spoke against Tiberius and his law.

By tradition, new laws were always proposed by the senate, then voted on by the people. Tiberius knew that the senators would never propose his law, so he called an assembly of the people and presented his law directly to them for a vote.

The senators saw this as an insult and a serious threat to their power. They convinced Marcus Octavius, another of the tribunes and a friend of Tiberius, to **veto** the law, which he did the next time the assembly met. Tiberius was a powerful and convincing speaker. He said, "The beasts have their dens, but the men who fight and risk their lives for their country's safety own nothing more in it but the air and light, and they wander from place to place with their children."

People and Terms to Know

veto—in Latin, the word means "I deny." If a tribune vetoed a law, it could not come before the people for a vote. Today, the word is used somewhat differently. A president can veto a law presented by Congress, but Congress can still pass the law if two thirds of the members vote for it.

Octavius hesitated, but remembering the powerful men he served, he continued his veto. Tiberius then made a decision that would destroy him. He argued that by vetoing a law that the people wanted, Octavius had failed to represent the people who had elected him and should be voted out of office. This was unheard of in Roman politics! After giving Octavius one more chance to change his mind, Tiberius called for the people's vote. Octavius was removed. With the threat of the veto gone, Tiberius's law passed easily.

The people were pleased with the law. However, they were uncomfortable with the fact that Tiberius had broken the customs of the republic. First, he had brought the law directly to them. Second, he had an elected tribune removed from office. The senate punished Tiberius in every way they could. They refused to give him a tent to use as he moved around the country enforcing the law, and they cut his pay.

Tiberius knew that once his year as tribune was over, the senate would charge him with what they called "unconstitutional" acts. So he asked the people to re-elect him for a second year. When the people gathered for the election, a senator who was still a friend warned Tiberius that the senators had voted to have him **assassinated**. Tiberius's supporters tucked their long gowns into their belts, broke apart the benches, and armed themselves, vowing to protect him. They failed. Tiberius and 300 of his supporters were killed, and their bodies were thrown in the Tiber River.

It is true that Tiberius had broken the customs of the republic, but the senate's response of assassination was also a first. Until then, disagreements had always been settled by discussion and compromise. This was a dangerous turn for the republic.

Gaius Gracchus was 20 years old when his brother was murdered in 133 B.C. At first Gaius did little. Some think that Tiberius's death had made Gaius choose a quiet life out of the public eye. According to legend, Tiberius appeared to his brother in a dream, and said, "Why do you delay, Gaius? There is no escape; one life and one death is appointed for us both, to spend the one and to meet the other in the service of the people."

Gaius reentered public life. He was a popular and hard-working officer. During one winter, the general he served ordered one Roman colony's

<hr>

People and Terms to Know

assassinated—murdered by surprise attack, usually for political reasons. The murder itself is called an *assassination*.

towns to provide warm clothing for the Roman soldiers. Several towns said that this was unfair, and the senate agreed. But this left the soldiers without warm clothing in the middle of winter. Gaius visited the towns and appealed to them for his men. He was well-liked, and the towns agreed to provide clothing for the soldiers.

Once again, a Gracchi brother had angered the senate! Senators worried about what would happen when Gaius returned and was elected to office. Their fears were justified. When Gaius was elected tribune, he insulted the senate. He faced the people when he spoke rather than facing away from them toward the senate, as was the custom. As he spoke, Gaius walked about, his robe swinging and his voice rising. Because he tended to become very emotional, particularly when talking about his brother's death, Gaius had a friend blow on a little flute if his voice became harsh or he drifted from the subject at hand. This only made him seem *more* different! The senators talked angrily among themselves about what should be done about Gaius.

▲

This painting from the 1700s shows the death of Gaius Gracchus.

Gaius not only supported Tiberius's land laws. He got the assembly to pass many other laws that helped the common people at the expense of the rich. He supervised the construction of roads and **granaries**. He wanted grain sold at a lower price to the poor. Other laws threatened to reduce the power of the senate even further. But the proposal that really angered the senate was one to give citizenship to all Italians. Roman citizens took pride in their privileged rights as citizens and didn't want to share them with "outsiders."

People and Terms to Know

granaries (GRAN•uh•reez)—buildings for storing grain.

Because of his popularity, Gaius was named to a second term as tribune. Winning a second term had resulted in his brother's death. Again, the senate feared a total loss of their power to the people. This time they decided to beat Gaius at his own game. When he proposed lowering the rent paid by poor people on land, the senators dropped the rent entirely. Whatever Gaius proposed, the senate accused Gaius of abusing the people and proposed something even more popular. Their promises were foolish, but all the senators cared about was winning the people's support away from Gaius.

In 121 B.C., Gaius failed to be elected tribune a third time. Now the Senate felt it was safe to destroy him. They said they were saving the republic from tyrants. They sent a group of armed men to kill Gaius and his supporters. Gaius's wife, holding their infant in her arms, begged him not to go to the assembly. "You go now unarmed to face to the murderers of Tiberius," she told him. "What trust can we place in the laws, or in the gods?" But he went, and Gaius and 3,000 of his followers were killed.

*　*　*

The deaths of the Gracchi marked a dangerous change in Roman politics. Now political conflicts were settled with violence. A century of disorder would follow that would lead to the end of the republic. Were the Gracchi responsible for the downfall of the Republic? Or were they reformers who truly wanted what was best for the people?

QUESTIONS TO CONSIDER

1. Why was the gap between Rome's rich and poor widening?
2. How did Tiberius Gracchus try to deal with this problem?
3. How were Tiberius and Gaius alike? How were they different?
4. Why did the senate fear the Gracchi?
5. To what extent do you think the Gracchi were responsible for the downfall of the Roman Republic?

Spartacus, Rebel Gladiator

BY MARIANNE McCOMB

The man in chains didn't even look up when he heard the rattle of keys at the cell door. It had been more than a week since he had seen another person, but he was not even curious. After all, he knew what was coming.

The man in chains was a **gladiator**. Gladiators fought to the death to entertain the crowds in the **amphitheaters** of the Roman Empire. These combats were held to mark important events, such as a victorious battle or a great man's funeral. This gladiator was one of many being trained at Batiatus's

---

People and Terms to Know

gladiator (GLAD•ee•AY•tuhr)—slave or paid fighter trained to fight other fighters or wild animals as public entertainment.

amphitheaters (AM•fuh•THEE•uh•tuhrs)—circular or oval buildings used as sports arenas. Some were large enough to hold 50,000 people.

Gladiators in the arena. One fighter is already dead, and another is about to be killed.

school in 73 B.C. The school was in **Capua**, a town in southern Italy near Mount Vesuvius. Some gladiators were slaves, some were criminals, and some were prisoners of war or deserters from the army.

Spartacus stood up and felt the same spark of anger that had been inside him for years.

In this school, there were gladiators who were taught to fight with a short sword and shield. Others learned to use a net and trident (a three-pointed spear). Gladiators fought each other or wild animals such as bears, lions, and bulls. When a wounded man fought well, the crowd sometimes spared him—it was thumbs up, let him live. Often it was thumbs down—kill him. Sometimes hundreds of gladiators died in a single fight.

"Get up, **Spartacus**," the guard growled. "On your feet, you lazy slave. You're wanted in the ring for today's fight."

Spartacus stood up and felt the same spark of anger that had been inside him for years. Once long ago, he had been a free and happy man living in the

People and Terms to Know

Capua (CAP•yoo•uh)—town south of Rome and a wealthy farming community. See the map on page 14.

Spartacus (SPAHR•tuh•kuhs)—gladiator from Thrace, a country on the Black Sea. He led a slave revolt in 73–71 B.C.

Roman colony of Thrace north of Greece. But Roman soldiers had captured him and dragged him to Capua to train as a gladiator.

Someday, though, he would return to his homeland, free once more. . . .

"Quit your daydreaming, Spartacus!" the guard ordered. He snapped an iron collar around Spartacus's neck. Next, he chained him to a group of 70 or so gladiators who were waiting in the hall.

Each of these men wanted to be free. Could they somehow help each other?

"Move on, slaves," the guard shouted. "We're off to the ring."

"Jupiter, help us all," a short man next to Spartacus mumbled.

The group of gladiators shuffled along behind the guard. They heard the roar of the crowd in the amphitheater. Spartacus ignored the crowd and looked at the other gladiators. Each of these men wanted to be free. Could they somehow help each other?

The guard pushed the gladiators against a wall outside the amphitheater. Then he ran off to tell Batiatus that the slaves were ready. Here was Spartacus's chance! In a low voice, he suggested a plan. As the first group of gladiators fought, the rest would make their escape, he explained. They would grab the guard who watched them and kill him quickly. Then they would take his keys and unlock themselves.

"Why should we do as you say, Spartacus?" a slave whispered. "We'll all be killed!"

Spartacus promised that his simple plan would not fail. Soon they would be free!

The guard returned and sat with his back to the slaves. For a moment, nothing happened. Then Spartacus cried out as if he were in pain. When the guard came over to look, two gladiators grabbed him and threw him to the ground. In a flash, the two had their hands around the guard's neck. They squeezed his throat until he was no longer breathing.

Working quickly, the slaves yanked at the guard's keys and unlocked each other. In less than five minutes, they were free!

Spartacus pushed the excited men back through the tunnel. They walked quickly but quietly. There were shadows on every wall and fear in the eyes of every man. Still they kept moving. There was no going back now!

Inside the amphitheater, one of the guards rushed over to Batiatus. "Master," the guard shouted to Batiatus. "The slaves have escaped! We saw Spartacus leading them through the tunnels!"

"Capture them, fool!" Batiatus roared. "They can't be far. And bring Spartacus to me. I'll throw him to the lions!"

* * *

Outside the school walls, Spartacus and the men stopped to rest. They could hear the shouts of the guards coming after them.

"Where will we go, Spartacus? They'll find us and kill us!" the slaves cried. Spartacus said that they would go north to Mount Vesuvius and hide there. So the men began to run.

"Come with us," they urged. "You can trust Spartacus! He will lead us to freedom!"

Along the way, they talked to all the slaves they could find. "Come with us," they urged. "You can trust Spartacus! He will lead us to freedom!" Many more slaves joined the fleeing gladiators. Soon hundreds marched behind Spartacus.

* * *

Almost a year later, in 72 B.C., the **Roman Senate** decided to do something about Spartacus. By this

People and Terms to Know

Roman Senate—group of officials who helped govern Rome.

time, nearly 70,000 slaves had joined him. The senate was angry that the slaves were still free. They were also angry that Spartacus's forces had been looting rich people's homes in the countryside. Finally, the Roman leaders were furious that the slaves had defeated Roman troops in three separate battles over the past year. For these reasons, the senate ordered a powerful Roman leader named **Marcus Licinius Crassus** to kill Spartacus and his men.

In 71 B.C., Spartacus and his men met Crassus and his troops in a great battle. The slaves fought fiercely, but the Romans finally defeated them. Thousands were killed. During the battle, Spartacus fought his way toward Crassus through showers of spears. Two Roman **centurions** attacked the gladiator, but he killed them both. Surrounded by his enemies, Spartacus bravely stood his ground and fought until he was killed. His body was never found.

After the battle, Crassus gathered 6,000 of the slaves and had them **crucified**. Their bodies were hung along the Appian Way, a road that extends

---

People and Terms to Know

Marcus Licinius Crassus—(c. 115–53 B.C.) charming, greedy, and powerful Roman leader. At one time, he was the richest man in Rome.

centurions (sehn•TUR•ee•uhns)—Roman army officers who commanded companies of 100 men.

crucified (kru•suh•FYD)—put to death by being hung upon a large wood cross until the lungs were crushed by the weight of the body. Death was by suffocation.

---

from Rome all the way to Capua. Crassus wanted the crucified men to be a lesson to all slaves. Although Spartacus was finally defeated, he has remained a symbol of resistance to slavery.

QUESTIONS TO CONSIDER

1. Who were the gladiators, and what did they do?

2. Why did the senate send Crassus to attack the slaves?

3. What signs of trouble in the Roman Republic does this story point out?

4. How would you argue for or against the Romans' right to punish the slaves in the way they did?

Gladiator's bronze helmet.
▼

Girlfight

Some women fought as gladiators. There is mention of a female gladiator in writing found in the ruins of the town of Pompeii. Some scientists think that the remains of a woman found buried in a Roman cemetery in London, England, may have been a gladiator. She was buried with a dish decorated with the image of a fallen gladiator and other things gladiators usually had.

See You Later, Gladiator
by Jon Scieszka

Jon Scieszka's comic novel describes the adventures of three boys who travel through time to ancient Rome and become students in a gladiator school.

Gladiator
by Richard Ross Watkins

In the beginning, most gladiators were prisoners of war, slaves, or criminals. Centuries later, gladiators had become so respected that many men volunteered to fight in the arenas of the Roman Empire. Richard Ross Watkins provides a complete introduction to the world of the Roman gladiators.

Running Out of Time
by Elizabeth Levy

In Elizabeth Levy's novel of time-travel, three friends running in the fog early one morning suddenly find themselves in Italy in 73 B.C. There they become part of the slave revolt led by the gladiator Spartacus.

Julius Caesar and His Friend Brutus

BY STEPHEN FEINSTEIN

Calpurnia begged Caesar to stay at home that morning. She had had such a horrible nightmare. She was so shaken that she could hardly talk about it. Yet she finally was able to tell her husband—she had seen blood flowing from a statue of Caesar! Now she was afraid something terrible would happen to Caesar if he went to the senate.

Seeing how upset she was, Caesar was tempted not to go. Then, he remembered the old soothsayer, the man who claimed to be able to tell the future. The soothsayer had told him "beware the Ides of March!" Today, March 15, was the Ides of March! **Julius Caesar**, the powerful ruler of Rome—the

---

People and Terms to Know

Julius Caesar (JOOL•yuhs SEE•zuhr)—(100–44 B.C.) Roman general, statesman, and historian.

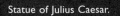
Statue of Julius Caesar.

most powerful person in the world—was not a superstitious man. And yet, perhaps there was something to all of this. Maybe he should pay attention to this warning. Caesar decided to stay home.

Meanwhile at the senate, everyone wondered where Caesar was. "It is not like him to arrive late," a senator called Lucius whispered to a friend. "You know how he likes to get right down to work, making all the decisions about almost everything." There was bitterness in Lucius's voice.

His friend, a man by the name of Marius, said, "Perhaps he is ill."

"Or perhaps he had too much wine to drink last night," said Lucius. "You know, I was a dinner guest at the house of Lepidus last night, and Caesar was there. As I said, the wine was flowing freely. I remember Caesar saying that a sudden death would be the best kind of death."

"Why did he say that?" asked Marius.

"Well, I don't know. At one point, for some reason, there was a discussion about death," said Lucius. "In any event, since Caesar was made dictator for life last October, he can do whatever he wants. Perhaps even make himself king of Rome. Do you remember what happened at the festival in the **forum** the other day? **Mark Antony** approached Caesar and placed a crown on his head."

"But the crowds did not cheer," said Marius. "And then Caesar removed the crown, pretending that he didn't want it. "

"Caesar was just testing the water, so to speak," said Lucius. "But I tell you, Caesar can become king if he chooses. I remember Caesar the conquering hero returning from **Gaul**. He showed off his captive **barbarians** in chains. The festivities and parades, the chariot races and gladiator fights—it went on for days on end."

"The crowds loved him," Marius said. "Caesar won the hearts of the **plebeians** by showering them with bread and circuses."

"My friend," said Lucius, "have you seen the new coins bearing Caesar's portrait? I'm afraid Caesar does plan to be king—king of Rome! And that means the days of the republic are over for us.

People and Terms to Know

forum—marketplace or public place in ancient Rome, in which courts of law met and public business was conducted.

Mark Antony (AN•tuh•nee)—(82–30 B.C.) Roman general and statesman; a friend of Caesar.

Gaul—ancient country of western Europe in the region occupied by present-day France.

barbarians (bahr•BAIR•ee•uhns)—people who lived beyond the borders of the Roman Empire and were considered by the Romans to be uncivilized.

plebeians (plih•BEE•uhns)—common people of ancient Rome.

You can say goodbye to our privileges. Now our words in government councils will mean little. Romans will no longer elect their rulers."

Other senators were saying similar things that morning in private conversations. Some among them seemed to be truly upset and were growing more so by the minute, although they tried to hide it. They had good reason to be nervous. Each one was carrying a dagger under his **toga**. They planned to plunge these daggers into Julius Caesar when he came into the senate! The plot had been organized by **Cassius**. He had carefully chosen only those Romans who had privately spoken of their great hatred for Caesar. Each had his own reasons for being against Caesar. Some felt that Caesar no longer showed them any respect. Others were angry at not being given a higher political rank. All feared a loss of power and importance. Cassius knew he could count on every one of them to carry out the plan. Cassius had not included Mark Antony. He believed Antony was probably too loyal to Caesar.

People and Terms to Know

toga (TOH•guh)—loose outer garment worn in public by citizens of ancient Rome.

Cassius (KASH•uhs)—(d. 42 B.C.) Roman general and leader of the plot against Caesar.

Among the plotters—60 in all—was **Brutus**, Cassius's brother-in-law. Cassius needed Brutus if the plan was to succeed. Romans, rich and poor, respected and liked Brutus. They believed him to be a serious statesman and a kind and thoughtful man. If Brutus was with them, the plotters' deed would appear to be a noble act to save the Roman Republic, not a murder to gain power.

Cassius needed Brutus if the plan was to succeed.

When Cassius had first asked Brutus, Brutus has said, "No!" Cassius was not surprised that Brutus didn't want to join the plot. Caesar and Brutus were close friends, although they had once been enemies. Indeed, Caesar had been very good to Cassius as well as to Brutus. Five years earlier, both Cassius and Brutus had served as officers under **Pompey**. They had fought against Caesar for control of Rome. Pompey's forces were beaten after a six-month-long civil war. Yet Caesar had spared the lives of Cassius and Brutus. He believed that pardons often turned former enemies into loyal

---

People and Terms to Know

Brutus—(85–42 B.C.) appointed governor of a Roman province in northern Italy by Caesar after the defeat of the general and consul Pompey.

Pompey (PAHM•pee)—(106–48 B.C.) Roman general and statesman.

followers. (Pompey, however, had escaped and was later murdered in Egypt.)

It had taken much convincing before Brutus agreed to join the plot. Time and again, Cassius and the others had begged him. "Think of the Roman Republic above all else." They appealed to him as a statesman to rise above personal feelings. Finally, Brutus saw the killing of Caesar as a necessary and noble act of sacrifice. With Brutus on their side, the plotters were ready to act.

"Send someone to Caesar's home," a senator suggested to Cassius, who himself was growing impatient. "Let's find out for certain whether he is ill."

Cassius sent another plotter, Decimus, to call on Caesar. Decimus noticed right away that Caesar did not appear to be ill.

"Caesar, the senate awaits your arrival," said Decimus with a puzzled look toward the worried Calpurnia. Caesar explained that he had decided to stay home to comfort his wife because she had had a bad dream.

At this, Decimus said to Caesar, "People will laugh and think you weak if I tell them this. They will gossip behind your back." Decimus kept urging that Caesar go to the senate immediately to put a stop to any rumors. He managed to change Caesar's mind.

As Caesar approached the senate, a Greek man who had heard about the plot slipped him a note. This Greek was a friend of Brutus, but his first loyalty was to Caesar. He begged Caesar to read the note quickly. Unfortunately, Caesar was distracted by the crowd in front of the senate and put the note aside. He intended to read it later. Caesar entered the senate alone. Caesar felt himself safe. He had survived attempts on his life and many close calls on the battlefield. He therefore believed he had no need of guards.

Caesar was quickly surrounded by the plotters. Brutus, however, hung back. Even now, having decided that Caesar's death was necessary, Brutus was torn by conflicting emotions. One moment, Caesar was his friend. The next, he was an enemy. Above all, he was the enemy of the Roman Republic. Then, no more time to think! One senator grabbed Caesar's toga and tugged it. This was the signal. Casca struck the first blow, stabbing Caesar in the neck from behind. A look of shock and anger crossed Caesar's face. The others closed in, twenty-three men slashing and stabbing with their daggers. In vain Caesar struggled, trying to fend them off, but he was growing weaker.

Suddenly, Caesar saw Brutus standing in front of him, dagger in hand, ready to strike. The last ounce of strength went out of him. Looking into his friend's face, Caesar said sadly, "*Et tu*, **Brute?**" as Brutus thrust the knife into his stomach. The man who would be king fell to the floor. Caesar's bloody body came to rest at the foot of Pompey's statue.

QUESTIONS TO CONSIDER

1. How did Caesar threaten the republic?

2. Why did his old friend Brutus finally believe Caesar's death was necessary?

3. What reasons did others have for killing Caesar?

4. What does Caesar's reason for sparing the lives of Cassius and Brutus tell you about Caesar?

5. If you had been a senator, what would you have done if asked to join the plot?

People and Terms to Know

"*Et tu*, **Brute?**"—The Latin words *et tu* mean "and you," but Caesar's last words are usually translated as "You too, Brutus?"

READING ON YOUR OWN

The Roman News
by Anthony Langley

"Caesar Stabbed," screams the headline on the cover of The Roman News, which presents life in ancient Rome in a the form of a daily newspaper written at the time.

Julius Caesar
by Robert Green

Robert Green's biography describes the rise and fall of Roman leader Julius Caesar.

Caesar's Conquest of Gaul
by Don Nardo

Caesar built his reputation as a military leader by conquering Gaul, the ancient region that is now France. Don Nardo describes the fierce 8-year military campaign in which the Romans defeated the Celtic inhabitants of Gaul.

Cleopatra, Egypt's Last Pharaoh

BY BARBARA LITTMAN

Cleopatra, still not 30 and quite a charmer of men, smiled to herself. All along the banks of the **Cydnus River**, people were gathering and running alongside her boat. This was just what she had hoped. When Mark Antony, one of three rulers of Rome, had asked her to go to the town of Tarsus, she had at first refused. She knew Antony wanted to talk to her about two things. First, he wanted her help in his war against **Parthia**. "Well, we'll see about that," she thought. Second, she knew he had

---

People and Terms to Know

Cleopatra (KLEE•uh•PAT•ruh)—(c. 69–30 B.C.) queen of ancient Egypt from 48 to 30 B.C.

Cydnus River (SIHD•nuhs)—river that ran by the city of Tarsus in Asia Minor. See map on page 70.

Parthia (PAHR•thee•uh)—ancient country in Asia, now in northeast Iran.

A Roman mosaic done shortly before Cleopatra's time shows boats on the Nile River.

heard rumors from her enemies. They were saying that she was involved in a plan for revenge against Caesar's murderers.

"Caesar!" she thought. How little it took to bring back memories of him. She still remembered the expression on his face when he saw her for the first time. She had come tumbling out of the carpet as her servant unrolled it in Caesar's room. Forced from the throne by her brother, Cleopatra knew she would need all her wits

She had set out to charm Caesar— and charm him she had.

and Caesar's help to get back her rightful place as ruler of Egypt. She had set out to charm Caesar—and charm him she had. Within a year she had her throne back, and Caesar was the father of her first child. Within two years, she and her son were living in Rome. Those days were gone now, but she still felt her heart beat fast when she thought of his murder. She would never forget her escape back to Egypt in the middle of the night. She had been afraid of what his murderers might do to her!

Cleopatra and Mark Antony had met in Rome. Caesar had trusted him and considered him a friend. Cleopatra liked him too, but she had learned

Cleopatra's World, 41–31 B.C.

that friendship was not enough. You must be clever and remain in control to succeed.

She had hesitated when Antony had summoned her to Tarsus, the city in Asia Minor where he was staying. After thinking it over, however, the clever Egyptian queen realized there was a way to turn this to her advantage. She did not want to come running as a mere subject of the Roman Empire. She was a **pharaoh**, a queen, even if Egypt was now ruled by

---

People and Terms to Know

pharaoh (FAIR•oh)—any of the rulers of ancient Egypt.

Rome. No, if she went to Tarsus, it would be on her terms. She would be the one in control, not Antony. So far, it looked as if things were going according to plan.

As her boat moved through the quiet water, people all along the shores cheered. They had never seen anything like it. Huge purple sails billowed in the wind. Silver oars dipped rhythmically in and out of the water. Music from stringed instruments drifted to shore. On deck, Cleopatra was dressed as the Greek goddess of love. She lay beneath an awning decorated with real gold. Surely this would get Antony's attention!

She lay beneath an awning decorated with real gold. Surely this would get Antony's attention!

Antony was in the marketplace when the noise began. It didn't take him long to understand what had happened. Caesar had warned him about Cleopatra. She may be a woman, but she had the mind of a politician. She is smart and wily as a fox, Caesar had warned.

Cleopatra had come to Tarsus as Antony had asked, but she had not set foot on Roman soil yet. Although Antony did not want to be outfoxed, he was basically a good-natured, fun-loving man. He agreed to Cleopatra's invitation to join her for dinner on her floating palace, though he knew this gave her the upper hand.

That night, Antony was fed and entertained as he had never been before. Musicians, singers, dancers, and a steady supply of food and drink were paraded before him, as was Cleopatra's charm. Before the evening was over, Antony had fallen in love.

Cleopatra appreciated Mark Antony. She knew he did not measure up to Caesar, the only other great love in her life. Still, Cleopatra thought she and Antony might be able to recapture the dream she and Caesar had had. They dreamed of ruling a Roman Empire that stretched from east to west.

While Cleopatra probably did set foot in Tarsus, she did not stay. Instead, she and Antony went to Alexandria, the capital of Egypt. What was to have been a short visit turned into a year. Finally, however, he had to return to Rome.

Antony spent three years in Rome, ruling with the other members of the **triumvirate**. During that time he had many disagreements with **Octavian**. When Antony left Rome, he traveled east to fight a

---

People and Terms to Know

triumvirate (try•UHM•vuhr•iht)—ruling body of three people.
Octavian (ahk•TAY•vee•uhn)—(63 B.C.–A.D. 14) one of three members of a triumvirate who ruled Rome. He later had the title of Augustus.

war against Parthia, a kingdom on the eastern border of the Roman Empire. He also sent for Cleopatra. When she arrived, he married her and asked her for money to fight his war.

Even though Antony won the war against Parthia, the people in Rome distrusted him more and more. They disapproved of his marriage to Cleopatra. Worse, they hated that he had given parts of the Roman Empire to his and Cleopatra's children.

Octavian asked the senate to declare war on Egypt. The senate agreed, but there were still many Romans who supported Antony. The leaders of other countries, including Syria and Greece, also supported Antony and Cleopatra. The ships of Cleopatra, Mark Antony, and their supporters gathered in a gulf near **Actium**. Soon, Octavian and his Roman fleet arrived and surrounded the opening of the gulf. They waited. The gulf was blocked and the ships of Antony and Cleopatra were trapped. Their food supplies were low, and the unhealthy climate made their men ill. Sick and discouraged, many soldiers deserted Antony to join Octavian.

People and Terms to Know

Actium (AK•shee•uhm)—piece of land that juts out into the Ionian Sea off the west coast of Greece.

Finally, Antony and Cleopatra prepared for battle. Antony's smaller ships rowed out and Cleopatra's large sailing ships followed. She didn't stay to help Antony fight, however. Instead, she turned her ships toward the open waters of the Mediterranean Sea and set sail for Egypt. Why she did this is a mystery. An even greater mystery is what Antony did. He abandoned his men and sailed after Cleopatra. Octavian soon overtook Antony's and Cleopatra's forces.

Some people say that Antony and Cleopatra had filled her ships with treasures and planned all along to abandon the battle. We will probably never know for sure, because it has been over 2,000 years since this happened in 31 B.C. What we do know is that this cowardice—or cunning—was the end of Cleopatra's dream to rule a large Roman Empire. For surely now, after his victory at Actium, Octavian would not even let her continue to rule Egypt.

Within a year, Octavian and his troops marched on Alexandria. Antony wanted to keep control of the city he now called home. He had land troops waiting and ships filled with warriors in the bay. Much to his surprise though, there was hardly any battle. Antony's sailors, tired of fighting, abandoned him almost immediately. They joined Octavian. When Antony's soldiers on land saw this, they did the same.

Antony couldn't believe his troops had deserted him. Cleopatra must have had made a deal with Octavian. He was furious. Cleopatra's servants warned her that Antony was angry. She fled to her tomb. Like all of Egypt's pharaohs, Cleopatra had had an elegant tomb built for herself. In this fortress-like building, Cleopatra kept jewels and other treasures. It was a perfect place to hide. Once it was closed, no one could get in.

Fearing for her life, Cleopatra hid in her tomb. She ordered her servants to tell Antony she was dead. When Antony heard this he collapsed in despair. He had lost much in the last few years. Now, he had lost the woman he loved. He had nothing more to live for. He drew his sword, placed the tip against his stomach, and fell forward.

When Cleopatra's servants reported to her that Antony was dead, she too was in despair. She knew Octavian wanted to capture her and parade her in chains through the streets of Rome. He had done the same to other leaders he had conquered. Cleopatra arranged for a small basket to be brought to her room. The basket was supposed to contain figs, but inside was really a small poisonous snake called an asp. Defeated and facing humiliation, she allowed the asp to crawl up her arm and bite her. Soon, the life of one of the most famous women in history was ended.

QUESTIONS TO CONSIDER

1. What was Cleopatra's dream?

2. Why did Rome, led by Octavian, turn against Mark Antony and Cleopatra?

3. Why did Antony lose the battle of Actium?

4. How did Cleopatra's behavior contribute to Rome's loss of a great leader, Mark Antony?

5. Why do you think Cleopatra has been remembered for 2,000 years?

This sculpture of Cleopatra was made while she was alive. ▶

Cleopatra

Cleopatra was the last of the Ptolemy (TAHL•uh•mee) family, Macedonians who ruled Egypt after the empire of Alexander the Great broke apart following his death in 323 B.C. Their rule came to an end when Cleopatra died in 30 B.C. She grew up in a family full of secrets and schemes and learned her political lessons well. Although she eventually brought ruin on herself, she was one of the most powerful women rulers the world has ever known.

READING ON YOUR OWN

Cleopatra
by Peter Vennema

Peter Vennema's biography provides an introduction to Cleopatra and her world.

Cleopatra VII:
Daughter of the Nile
by Kristiana Gregory

Kristiana Gregory's historical novel about the young Cleopatra describes her struggles to survive the plottings of the other members of the royal family.

Cleopatra:
Goddess of Egypt, Enemy of Rome
by Polly Schoyer Brooks

Patty Schoyer Brooks's biography presents the life of the Egyptian queen against the background of Rome's struggle for control of the Mediterranean World.

The Empire

Caesar Augustus

BY WALTER HAZEN

He wasn't the healthiest Roman I'd ever known. He suffered from diseases of the joints and the bladder. His skin was so sensitive that the frequent itch made his life miserable. In winter, he had to wear a woolen chest protector, four tunics (shirts), and a heavy toga to stay warm. He had trouble sleeping, and he ate very little.

Doesn't sound much like a mighty ruler, does he? Yet he was. "He" was Caesar Augustus. Before becoming **Imperator Augustus**, he was simply Octavian. He was the grandnephew of Julius

---

People and Terms to Know

Imperator Augustus (IHM•puh•RAH•tawr aw•GUHS•tuhs)—first Roman emperor. He ruled from 27 B.C. to A.D. 14. The word *imperator* meant "conqueror." In time, it evolved into *emperor*.

This marble statue of Augustus in military uniform was put up around A.D. 20, a few years after his death. His bare feet signify he is a god. His right arm is extended, as if he were addressing his soldiers.

Caesar. Many people believe he was Caesar's adopted son. He was 18 years old when Caesar was killed that sad day in Rome. The events that followed form the basis of my story.

Let me introduce myself. My name is Favius. For many years, I was a minor official in the government of Augustus. My family was not rich nor important. On the contrary, my father was of the middle class. But that is the way Augustus did things. Many people who served in his government were from the lower classes. Some were even former slaves.

Back to my story. When Caesar was killed, Octavian was studying in Greece. He immediately returned to Rome to claim the power he thought was rightfully his. But he soon discovered that he had a rival in Mark Antony. Antony had been a close associate of Caesar's and considered himself in line to succeed him.

To keep the peace, Octavian and Antony formed a triumvirate (group of three) with Marcus Lepidus. Lepidus was the powerful governor of one of Rome's colonies. The three men agreed that Octavian would rule in the west and Antony in the east. Lepidus would take control of Roman lands in North Africa.

I was not surprised when Lepidus quickly faded from the picture. He always struck me as the least forceful of the three. His fall from power left Octavian and Antony to fight it out for control of the empire. (We did not yet have an emperor. However, Rome had conquered so many lands that we were already an empire.)

Octavian quickly became the favorite of the people of Rome. This was because he succeeded in turning many Romans against

Octavian quickly became the favorite of the people of Rome.

Antony. To be honest, Antony brought his troubles on himself. As ruler of the east, his territory included Egypt, a country ruled by a sly queen named Cleopatra.

Cleopatra was a strong-willed woman who considered herself equal to Rome's governors. The fact that Egypt had been made a part of the Roman empire mattered little to her. Earlier, Julius Caesar had made a fool of himself over her. Then, about seven years later, Mark Antony did the same.

Two things about Antony upset Octavian. First, he suspected that Antony and Cleopatra were plotting to set up an empire of their own. Second, Antony had left his wife in favor of the Egyptian queen. The reason this bothered Octavian is obvious. Antony's wife was Octavia, the sister of Octavian. Seeing his sister pushed aside for a "foreigner" didn't sit well with big brother Octavian.

Everyone in Rome knew a showdown was in the making. They didn't have long to wait. With a navy of 400 ships and an army numbering about 90,000, Octavian set out for Egypt. He defeated the forces of Antony and Cleopatra at Actium, a **cape** off western Greece.

Octavian returned to Rome a hero. Now he was in complete control. The senate granted him all sorts of titles. One was *princeps*, or "first citizen." Another was *imperator*, or "conqueror." He became officially known as Caesar Augustus. "Augustus" was an ancient title of honor. Whether the senate or Octavian himself came up with "Augustus" has always been open to argument. The same goes for the calendar month August. Some Romans say Augustus insisted on the eighth month being named for him.

People and Terms to Know

cape—piece of land jutting out into the water.

Caesar Augustus was thirty-six when he began his **reign**. I was the same age when I was appointed to office. In spite of his health, Augustus threw himself into his work with great energy. He was proud that, as he boasted, he had "found Rome a city of brick and left it one of marble."

In addition to his interest in architecture, Augustus also encouraged some of our greatest artists and writers. Among the writers were Virgil and Horace. I think Virgil will always be remembered for his splendid long poem, the _Aeneid_.

Augustus never wore a crown. He also never called himself a king or an emperor. Although he had supreme power, he wanted people to believe that he had made Rome a republic once again. He showed this by giving respect to senators and by seeking their advice on important issues.

Augustus may never have been officially crowned, but his accomplishments rivaled that of any king or emperor. During his reign, our

---

People and Terms to Know

reign (rayn)—years a ruler is in power.
Aeneid (ih•NEE•ihd)—Virgil's long poem about the hero Aeneas. Romulus and Remus, legendary twins of early Rome, were said to be Aeneas's grandsons.

empire stretched from Spain in the west to the Euphrates River in the east, and from the Rhine and Danube rivers in the north to Egypt in the south. I personally think, however, that his greatest achievement was in bringing peace. Rome has not experienced war or revolution in forty-six years!

The family of the Roman emperor Augustus.
▼

Five years have passed since Augustus died. As for myself, I am now a retired gentleman of 81. On warm summer days, I like to sit outside my country home and think of the exciting life I have led. Often, my thoughts turn to Augustus. When they do, I think about how fortunate I was to have served under such an outstanding ruler.

QUESTIONS TO CONSIDER

1. What relation was Octavian to Julius Caesar?

2. How might history have been different had Antony and Cleopatra won out over Octavian?

3. Why do you think Augustus wanted Romans to believe he had brought back the Republic?

4. Why do you think Rome was ready to accept Augustus as a supreme ruler?

Ancient Rome:
A Guide to the Glory of Imperial Rome
by Jonathan Stroud

Augustus boasted, "I found Rome a city of bricks and left it a city of marble." Jonathan's Stroud's book is a guide to Rome as it was in the days of the empire.

Augustus and Imperial Rome
by Miriam Greenblatt

Miriam Greenblatt introduces the life and reign of Augustus Caesar. She also describes everyday life in Rome during the time of Augustus.

Augustus Caesar's World: 44 B.C. to A.D. 14
by Genevieve Foster

Genevieve Foster's full account of the life of Augustus Caesar also describes important events in the rest of the world.

Who Killed Claudius?

BY JUDITH LLOYD YERO

Tragedies! Plots! Murders! Unfaithful wives, wicked stepmothers, and scheming stepchildren!

This may sound like the perfect plot for a soap opera or fairy tale. In reality, it is the true story of the fourth Roman emperor, **Claudius**. Born in the year 10 B.C., Claudius's full name was Tiberius Claudius Drusus Nero Germanicus.

His name was the only impressive thing about the young Claudius. His family included the great Roman emperor Augustus, and the general Mark Antony. But Claudius did not fit the royal mold.

People and Terms to Know

Claudius (KLAW•dee•uhs)—(10 B.C.–A.D. 54) ruler of the Roman Empire from A.D 41 to 54. Claudius succeeded to the throne after the assassination of Caligula. He increased the empire through the conquest of Britain. He also built public works and gave citizenship to many people from outlying provinces.

A sculpture of Claudius made in A.D. 41, the year he became emperor.

Either from birth defects or an early childhood illness, Claudius had a number of minor physical problems. In the words of one biographer of the early Roman emperors, Claudius looked fine as long as he stood still. "But when Claudius walked, his weak knees gave way under him and he had many disagreeable traits. . . . He would foam at the mouth and trickle at the nose; he stammered besides and his head was very shaky at all times."

Claudius was an embarrassment to his family and was kept out of the public eye.

Romans respected strength. People with physical problems were considered stupid and worthless. Therefore, Claudius was an embarrassment to his family and was kept out of the public eye.

Claudius's luck with marriage and family wasn't much better. His engagement at the age of 15 was called off when the bride's parents fell out of favor with the court. His next attempt at marriage ended when the bride died on her wedding day. He divorced his first wife, Plautia, because she was unfaithful to him and was suspected of murder.

Their son later choked on a pear after throwing it in the air and trying to catch it in his mouth.

Claudius divorced a second wife in order to marry **Valeria Messalina**, a beautiful young girl from a well-known family. Claudius was 50 at the time and still a "hanger-on" in the court. With no royal demands on his time, Claudius read constantly and wrote over 70 books on history. He even wrote his own life story in 8 volumes. You might wonder what he had done to rate such a long autobiography!

By now, Claudius's nephew, **Caligula**, was emperor. Caligula was cruel and loved to make fun of Claudius. As a joke, he named the stammering Claudius as consul, a chief advisor. That didn't mean much because he had once named his horse to the same position!

Tired of Caligula's cruelty, members of the **Praetorian Guard** killed the emperor in A.D. 41. Claudius was the only male member of the royal family left. At first, he feared that the soldiers would kill

---

People and Terms to Know

Valeria Messalina (vuh•LEER•ee•uh MEHS•uh•LYN•uh)—(A.D. 22–48) third wife of Claudius. She and Claudius had two children.

Caligula (kuh•LIHG•yuh•luh)—emperor of Rome (A.D. 37–41). He was a ruthless, wasteful leader. He once made his soldiers fill their helmets with seashells, declaring himself victor over the gods of the sea.

Praetorian (pree•TAWR•ee•uhn) **Guard**—soldiers who guarded the life of the emperor; bodyguards.

him, too. Instead, they named him emperor! Some have suggested that Claudius wasn't all that innocent. He may have plotted with the soldiers to kill his evil nephew. It's also possible that the soldiers believed Claudius was so stupid that they could control him.

Claudius was no fool. He understood that it was the strength of the army and not the wishes of the Roman Senate that kept an emperor in power. Claudius immediately gave the soldiers a gift of money to insure their loyalty. When members of the senate tried to have Claudius removed, their own soldiers joined Claudius's troops. Money talks!

As emperor, Claudius tried to appeal to all sides. First, he had Caligula's killers put to death. Then, he threw out all of the hated laws that Caligula had passed when he was in power. Claudius was trying to let the senate and the people see that he was not like his nephew.

Because Claudius was not the senators' choice for emperor, plots against his life were common. More than 35 senators and 300 other people were executed during his reign for suspected plots or attempts to kill him. Unfortunately, Claudius's wife Messalina was behind some of those plots.

Claudius and Messalina had two children, a daughter, Octavia, and a son, Britannicus. As

▲

Remains of a Roman aqueduct in Spain. Usually, the water channels of aqueducts were at ground level or below. But when there was a need to cross low ground, the water channel was raised on high arches.

mother of the future emperor, Messalina thought her position was secure. She was a ruthless and powerful empress. Known for her beauty, she teased and flirted with everyone from senators to actors, often having them killed if they resisted her advances or threatened her position.

Finally Messalina went too far, even for the mild-mannered Claudius. While Claudius was away, she threw a huge party and openly "married" one of Claudius's rivals. That was enough! Messalina was killed, along with her new "husband." Once again, Claudius was without a wife.

Despite the soap-opera qualities of his life, Claudius did several important things for the Roman Empire. He led a successful attack on Britain in A.D. 43—adding this important colony to the empire. He completed an **aqueduct** begun by Caligula and built another, the Aqua Claudia. This greatly increased Rome's water supply. He expanded the harbor of Ostia, ending the grain shortages that had been a problem in Rome for years.

In A.D. 49, Claudius married his niece, **Agrippina the Younger**. Agrippina already had a son, **Nero**. Nero was a few years older than Claudius's own son, Britannicus. Agrippina convinced Claudius to adopt Nero. No one is sure why Claudius agreed, but he did indeed treat Nero as his son. As Nero became a young man, Claudius allowed him to

---

People and Terms to Know

aqueduct (AK•wih•DUHKT)—channel used to carry water from the mountains to the cities and surrounding farmlands.

Agrippina (AG•ruh•PY•nuh) **the Younger**—(c. A.D. 15–59) Roman empress, fourth wife of Claudius and mother of the emperor Nero.

Nero (NEE•roh)—(A.D. 37–68) emperor of Rome from A.D. 54 to 68. He may have set the great fire of Rome in 64.

address the senate. He had Nero's picture put on coins. Britannicus received no such honors.

Agrippina was another powerful empress, receiving important foreigners in her own private court. She became so powerful that the senate even added the title of Augusta (empress) to her name.

In A.D. 53, at the age of 16, Nero was married to Claudius's daughter, Octavia. This assured that he would be the next emperor—whenever Claudius died. Agrippina speeded up that process. According to most accounts, she fed Claudius poisonous mushrooms. When Claudius only became ill, she kept on trying. She convinced the doctor who treated him to help her, and Claudius did indeed die in A.D. 54. Nero was now emperor.

Claudius once stated that it was his destiny first to suffer and finally to punish the wickedness of his wives. Agrippina's punishment came after his death. At her urging, he cleared the way for Nero to be emperor. As emperor, Nero finally got tired of Agrippina's attempts to boss him. After several failed attempts, using collapsing ceilings and collapsing boats, Nero finally had his mother killed. Though long dead, Claudius got his revenge.

Pumpkin Becomes a God

Most Roman emperors were honored as gods after their deaths. At their funerals there was an official ceremony that made them into gods. After the emperor Claudius died, the Roman writer Seneca wrote a work called Pumpkin Becomes a God.

The "pumpkin" is Claudius. Seneca thought he was a fool. According to Seneca, when Claudius arrives in heaven, the gods can't find out who he is at first because of his stammer. Then the emperor Augustus says that Claudius should be punished in the underworld because he had so many people killed. In the underworld, Claudius is beaten by his nephew Caligula and then forced to be the servant of one of his own former slaves. Seneca feels this is what ought to happen to this "god."

QUESTIONS TO CONSIDER

1. Why was Claudius never given royal duties until Caligula died?
2. How did Claudius eventually become emperor?
3. What things did Claudius do for the Roman Empire?
4. If you had been a member of the Roman senate, what would you have thought about Claudius as an emperor?

Paul Spreads Christianity

BY LYNNETTE BRENT

Our ship set sail from **Caesarea** in the fall. The sun was still warm, but a cool breeze made me think that our entire sea journey would not be taken in warm weather. I was to guard and escort a number of prisoners to Rome. Among the group was a man named **Paul**. He had traveled about teaching people about someone named Jesus. I felt bad for Paul. I had heard that he was about to be freed when he asked for a hearing before the emperor in

---

People and Terms to Know

Caesarea (SEE•zuh•REE•uh)—ancient Roman capital of Judea (now Israel). Judea was part of the Roman Empire. See the map on page 70.

Paul—Jew and Roman citizen who was an early convert to Christianity. He established Christian churches in many countries and wrote most of the epistles (or letters) in the New Testament of the Bible. He was born in Tarsus about A.D. 10 and died about A.D. 67.

Early Christians used the halls and rooms of underground cemeteries to hide from their enemies. In this one in Rome, they held religious services.

Rome. Then he had to endure a long voyage, as well as appearing before the emperor.

The followers of Jesus were called Christians. Paul was a Christian, and we Romans are very nervous about Christians. We have our own religion. The Christians don't fit in. Their customs and ideas are different from ours.

Paul was arrested in **Jerusalem**. I heard on the streets in Caesarea that a group of **Jews** had attacked him. He was moved to Caesarea for protection. Whatever crimes he committed in Jerusalem were handled at a trial in Caesarea. The rumors were that he was imprisoned wrongly. Nevertheless, we had started on our way to see the emperor Nero. I was curious to learn more about this man named Paul.

Our voyage began peacefully. Unfortunately, we soon sailed into terrible weather. Strong winds tugged at the sails. Suddenly we were in real danger. The storms pounded and tossed the ship. We

---

People and Terms to Know

Jerusalem (juh•ROO•suh•luhm)—ancient city in Judea that had been the capital of the Jewish kingdom, conquered by the Romans.

Jews—descendants of the ancient Israelites. Judaism was a major religion throughout the Roman Empire.

were afraid that the ship would sink, so the sailors threw much of the cargo overboard. They were trying to make the ship as light as possible. We drifted for days. We had no idea where we were. The soldiers on the ship didn't want the prisoners to escape. Instead, they suggested that the prisoners be killed. I argued until they agreed to spare the prisoners' lives. Finally we all reached land. The people of the area were kind. We had food and shelter to get us through the winter. We were there for months.

It was during this stay that I came to know Paul better. I talked to him about my life, and he told me about his. He was a faithful Jew. He had felt so strongly about his faith that he sought out and captured followers of Jesus. Paul, and many other Jews, felt that Jesus had taught ideas that went against their laws. One day, Paul saw a bright light and heard the voice of Jesus. Blinded by the light, Paul went to Damascus, a city in Syria. A follower of Jesus helped him see again. Then Paul became a believer in Jesus. He committed his life to teaching Jews and others about Christianity. A group of Jews put him in prison and plotted to kill him. Some

Christians managed to help Paul escape from prison in Damascus by sneaking him through an opening in the city wall. They lowered him to the ground in a large basket.

After escaping from Damascus, Paul traveled throughout the Roman Empire. He was able to convert many Jews to Christianity. He brought many non-Jews to the new faith as well. One group of Jews, called the Pharisees (FAR•ih•seez), was particularly angry about Paul. They were strict followers of Jewish law. Paul's ideas were in conflict with many of those Jewish laws. This group viewed Paul as a bitter enemy.

As a Roman centurion, I know that the government normally lets these religious conflicts go on without getting involved. We don't worry about such a conflict until it causes an uprising or rioting. Unfortunately, it did not take long for riots to start when Paul came around. He was attacked by both Jews and Romans.

It is hard to imagine this man causing such a stir. He was by no means threatening. After all his travels, he looked tired. He clearly had injuries from the attacks on him. Paul looked more like a beggar than a threat to the empire.

I was strange to think of Paul as a Roman citizen, but he was. Not everyone could become a citizen, and many people chose not to be. I doubt that Paul lived as a Roman, but being a citizen did have its benefits. A Roman citizen could have someone speak for him if he were ever charged with a crime. This person could argue, pray, cry, and even offer money to help the prisoner receive better treatment. Unfortunately, nobody would speak for Paul. In the past, Paul was able to convince the Romans that he was innocent

It was strange to think of Paul as a Roman citizen, but he was.

of the charges that were brought against him. At the very least, he should have been spared some forms of execution—such as crucifixion—because of his citizenship.

Things have changed now. Rome was set on fire in A.D. 64. What a day that was! Many temples, homes, and businesses were destroyed. Nero made it clear that he thought that Christians had set the fire.

Once we had brought the prisoners to Rome, I was no longer responsible for watching over Paul. Still, I was interested to know what would happen. I visited him when I could.

Paul was taken before the emperor Nero and a number of judges to plead his case. Instead of begging for his life or arguing, however, Paul told them about the teachings of Jesus.

Nero didn't act right away. Instead he simply imprisoned Paul. Paul was allowed to write letters to his followers, and he received some visitors. When I saw him last he looked much older. Nero was punishing Christians in horrible ways. Some were torn to death by dogs. Others were used as human torches at the emperor's parties. I feared what Nero had planned for Paul.

The last time I went to see Paul, he was gone. No one could tell me what had happened to him, and I was afraid to ask questions. If the government thought I was a Christian, I would certainly lose more than my job. I still think about that brave man, however.

QUESTIONS TO CONSIDER

1. What made the Romans decide to interfere with Paul and his teachings?
2. What were the advantages of being a Roman citizen?
3. Why do you think Nero made it clear that Christians had set the fire that burned Rome?
4. How can one person who is not a ruler be a threat to an empire?

A Soldier's Life

BY STEPHEN FEINSTEIN

The Roman soldiers sat around the campfire eating dinner. The sun had just set and a cool breeze had sprung up. It brought relief from the heat of the day. The men were exhausted. The battle that day against the **Parthians** had not gone well. The bodies of dead Roman soldiers were piled thick in the river that ran through the middle of the valley. More than half of the six thousand soldiers in the **legion** had died. The Romans were hopelessly outnumbered by the Parthians.

Quintus sat by himself at the edge of the camp, away from the others. He had removed his metal

---

People and Terms to Know

Parthians—inhabitants of the Parthian Empire (ancient Persia) in what is now Iran.

legion—company of 3,000 to 6,000 foot soldiers and 300 to 700 men on horseback.

These Roman soldiers served under the emperor Hadrian, who ruled from A.D. 117 to 138.

armor, carefully placing it on the ground next to his helmet, sword, dagger, and shield. It was a relief to wear only his woolen tunic. The heavy armor with its metal strips, and leather straps on the inside, weighed him down. In the flickering campfire light, Quintus thought about his beloved wife Tullia. He had not seen her in more than two years. And now, he had a sinking feeling that he might never see her again. In fact, he was afraid that the very next day might be his last. Roman scouts had just returned to camp with word that thousands of fresh troops had arrived in the Parthian camp. Quintus knew that the closest new Roman troops were at least a five-day march away.

Quintus looked out across the valley into the darkness. It was very peaceful. He could see the Parthian campfires twinkling like stars on the hillsides. He tried not to think about the terrible events of the day. He thought, instead, about the last time he had seen his sons. Cilnius (SIHL•nee•uhs) was just beginning to talk, and little Marcus was just beginning to walk. Quintus imagined that if he lived to see them again, he would hardly recognize them. It saddened him that he had been so far away from home for such a long time. If only he could send his family a message. He would tell them how much he missed them and loved them.

Quintus would have liked to have gone on thinking about Tullia and the boys. But try as he might, he could not keep images of the day's battle out of his mind. Once again Quintus saw the river that ran red with blood. Again, he heard the cries of the wounded and dying soldiers. For hours the Romans had battled the Parthians in hand-to-hand combat. They had swung their swords until their arms went numb. Meanwhile, wave after wave of armor-piercing arrows had rained down on them from the Parthian archers on the hillsides. Amidst the shouting and confusion, Quintus had seen his two closest friends cut down. Filled with fury, Quintus leaped at the Parthians, plunging his sword into the nearest one. He narrowly escaped death the next moment. He ducked aside just in time to avoid a spear aimed at him.

For hours the Romans had battled the Parthians in hand-to-hand combat.

Quintus considered what was likely to happen to him the next day. He also reviewed the path that had led him here. Quintus, and many others like him, had joined Rome's legions. It was the only job they could find. They were among the poorest of Romans. They had grown up in the slums of Rome or in poverty in the countryside. The work of a Roman soldier was dangerous and difficult. Many died or suffered horrible wounds. They fought Rome's enemies all along the far-flung borders of the Roman Empire. But Quintus earned enough money to send some back to his family. And there was always the possibility that he could work his way up in the ranks and become an officer. But he would never become a centurion nor a general. They usually came from wealthy families.

Quintus had gone from one campaign to the next, doing as he was told. He understood that armies were necessary. They protected the empire from its enemies along the borders. He had been perfectly content to let the politicians and generals concern themselves with the glory of Rome. Such fancy ideas didn't concern Quintus. He was just doing his job. Then Emperor **Trajan** decided to expand the empire eastward and conquer the land of the Parthians. As if Rome didn't have enough land to worry about! Quintus wasn't the only one beginning to question the wisdom of Trajan's policy. This much Quintus knew. Trajan had defeated the **Dacians** by A.D. 109. It was an eight-year-long campaign, and Quintus had taken part. Some years later, the emperor looked east-ward. He extended the borders of Rome to the Euphrates and added Arabia to the empire. (See the map on page 14.) This brought the Romans closer to the borders of the Parthian Empire. At the time, there was an uneasy peace between the Romans and their old enemies the Parthians. But then, a quarrel arose over Armenia. Armenia was on the border between both empires. For many years, the Romans and Parthians had a deal. The Parthians chose Armenia's king, but the king was officially granted his throne by the Romans.

There was an uneasy peace between the Romans and their old enemies the Parthians.

People and Terms to Know

Trajan—(A.D. 53–117) Roman emperor, A.D. 98–117.
Dacians (DAY•shuns)—inhabitants of Dacia. See the map on page 14.

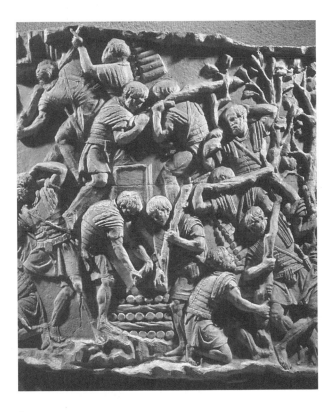

▲
Roman soldiers had to be able to build as well as fight.

In A.D. 113, the Parthians chose an Armenian king without Rome's approval. Trajan was outraged. He sent his legions into Armenia and began a war. After quickly conquering Armenia, Trajan pushed eastward into the heart of the Parthian Empire. When he attacked the capital city, the Parthian king fled. Roman legions swept across much of Parthia. Within a year they had reached as far as the Persian Gulf. But no sooner had Trajan declared Parthia a Roman state, when the Parthian king reappeared at the head of a huge army. The Romans began to lose control of Parthian lands. Quintus knew that at least one Roman general and his legion had been wiped out. Rebellions broke out in other Roman provinces in the east, such as Syria. Trajan's forces were now stretched too thin over too vast an area. To Quintus and other Roman soldiers, Trajan's conquest of Parthia began to seem like a big mistake.

Once again, Quintus's thoughts turned to his wife and children. If he did die in tomorrow's battle, he hoped his death would not be in vain. He hoped that the next emperor would learn from Trajan's mistakes. If only this emperor would decide to make the empire a better place instead of a bigger place. A world at peace—that was the kind of world Quintus wished for his sons. Cilnius and Marcus would not have to follow in his footsteps when they grew up. There would be no soldier's life for them.

QUESTIONS TO CONSIDER

1. Why was Quintus gloomy about the outcome of the Roman army's battle against the Parthians?

2. Why did Quintus enlist in the Roman army?

3. In what way did Quintus's outlook differ from that of the politicians and generals?

4. What was Quintus's opinion of Emperor Trajan's policy regarding Parthia?

5. What kind of world did Quintus wish for his sons?

The Roman Army
by John Wilkes

John Wilkes explains how the Roman army was organized during the time of the empire and what the daily life of a Roman soldier was like.

The Legionary
by Peter Connolly

Peter Connolly uses a variety of historical materials to reconstruct the career of a Roman soldier serving on the Danube frontier.

The Eagle of the Ninth
by Rosemary Sutcliff

Rosemary Sutcliff's historical novel tells the story of Marcus Aquila, a young centurion serving in Roman Britain. Marcus must go among the hostile tribes beyond the Roman Wall. His goal is to recover the eagle standard of the Ninth, a legion which mysteriously disappeared under his father's command.

Daily Life in Ancient Rome

The Appian Way

BY STEPHEN CURRIE

Footsteps sounded on the hard surface of the **Appian Way** near Capua. Inside the inn that bore his name, Calumnus yawned and stretched. The rain and fog had lasted all day and kept even the hardiest travelers away. Here, at last, was a customer.

"Good evening!" Calumnus said, throwing open the heavy wooden door. "Welcome to the Calumnus Inn! Been traveling long?" Well, of course the man had, he reminded himself. There were no buildings or crossings for dozens of _stadia_

People and Terms to Know

Appian (AP•ee•uhn) **Way**—first major road in Roman territory. When the original construction was finished in the third century B.C., the road ran from Rome south to the town of Capua. See the map on page 14. Later it was extended to the town of Brindisi, further south. Some parts of the Appian Way are still in use today.

stadia—plural of _stadium_, Roman unit of distance equal to about 600 feet.

up the road. There was nothing but Appius Claudius's old tomb, in fact.

"Long enough," agreed the visitor, entering the inn and taking a seat. His toga and sandals were grand, almost regal, but quite old-fashioned, Calumnus noticed. At least, he thought, my clothes are stylish, and he pulled his brand-new tunic proudly around his chest.

"Fix you something to eat?" Calumnus asked.

"And a hot drink? And a room for the night?" He hoped the answers would be Yes, Yes, and Yes. "As **Horace** said, 'The Appian Way is less tiring to those who are not in a hurry.'"

"Horace?" The visitor raised his eyebrows quizzically.

"The poet." Calumnus tried not to laugh. Surely the visitor knew of Horace. Horace had died many years before, but his fame lived on.

"Ah," murmured the visitor, looking blank. "Just something to drink, thanks. I'll soon be on my way again."

"Of course," said Calumnus, disappointed but trying not to show it. He turned and began to heat the wine.

People and Terms to Know

Horace—Roman poet of the first century B.C. Among his writings was a description of a trip he made along the Appian Way.

"Has this inn been here long?" the guest asked, looking around the room. Wisps of fog floated past the windows.

"It's the oldest inn on the Appian Way," Calumnus said proudly. "It was founded hundreds of years ago by the original Calumnus, my ancestor, back when the road was just being built. Of course, we've added many modern conveniences over the years," he added quickly, in case the stranger should think that everything was just the way it had been several centuries earlier.

Thunder rumbled in the distance. "I thought it seemed familiar," the stranger said. "Nice place."

Calumnus loved to tell his visitors about the Appian Way.

Calumnus's heart swelled. "Well. Yes, of course. I mean—thank you. Maybe you'd like me to tell you about the road," he added quickly, suddenly embarrassed.

Calumnus loved to tell his visitors about the Appian Way. In his view, the system of roads had made Rome what it was. Today, roads ran from Rome to the farthest outposts of the empire—Spain,

Arabia, Africa, Britain. Roads were for soldiers and traders and ordinary travelers—for everyone! And it had begun right here on the Appian Way.

The stranger dipped his hand into the bowl of figs Calumnus kept on the table and popped two into his mouth. "Please."

"A man named **Appius Claudius** first had the idea to build this road," Calumnus began as he had so many times. "That's why it was called the Appian Way. It's Appius's Road, right? Appius was a censor. He was a great man. Have you heard of him?"

"You could say that." A flicker of a smile crossed the visitor's face.

"They started construction early in his term of office," continued Calumnus as he checked the wine. "Do you know how they built the road?"

"Tell me." The stranger sat back. Outdoors, lightning flashed.

Calumnus always thought roadbuilding was much like cooking, only the recipe involved stones

---

People and Terms to Know

Appius Claudius—man who directed the beginning of construction on the Appian Way in the fourth century B.C. A censor, or Roman government official, Appius Claudius went blind late in life. When he died, he was buried in a tomb beside the roadway that was named for him.

and mortar, not flour and honey. "Dig a trench twenty feet wide," he explained. "Line it with big flat stones. Mix lime, gravel, and sand; fill. Arrange volcanic rocks to form pavement. Congratulations! You have a road."

"Very clever," the stranger said, helping himself to another fig. "These figs are delicious."

"They came in on the roads," Calumnus said proudly. "Wonderful things, roads. Anyway, Appius Claudius ordered this road built. Did you happen to pass his tomb? It's just a little ways north of here. You probably missed it in the rain and fog—"

"I'm—familiar with it," said the stranger. "How long did it take to complete the road?"

Calumnus placed his hand over the warming wine, then took a small sip. Yes, it was ready. "Nearly seventy years," he said, pouring the hot drink into a cup for his guest. "First they built the 132-mile stretch from Rome to Capua. Later they continued it another two hundred miles to Brindisi. Terrific road!" He smiled. "Have you traveled it before?"

"Not for years," the stranger smiled back, "but it's still in great shape."

Calumnus beamed with pride. "This is the best road in the empire," he said. "Why, it's just as strong as when Appius had it built. Never needs repair. Ask anybody."

"I take your word." The stranger drank deeply from his cup.

"The sad thing is that Appius never saw the completed road," Calumnus went on. "Most of the road was built after his death. And even before his death, he didn't actually see the road. He went blind, you know." He held up a finger. "When he was an old man, though, Appius walked the road anyway. He did it barefoot. He couldn't see it, but he could feel it." He paused. "I'm sure he enjoyed it. Still, I wish he'd seen it."

"Me, too," agreed the stranger, and he raised his cup in a toast. "To Appius!"

"To Appius," echoed Calumnus. Thunder rolled outside.

His guest stood. "I must be going," he said. "Thank you for the stories and the wine." He flipped a coin toward Calumnus.

"You're heading out?" Calumnus cried, catching the coin in his left hand. A gust of wind flung open the door. "This night's not fit for a person to be traveling."

The visitor's eyes twinkled. "It may not be fit for a person out there, but I'm not technically a person any more. I haven't been for centuries."

Calumnus's heart gave a lurch, and all at once things began to fall into place. The old-fashioned clothes. The visitor's ignorance of Horace. Some of the comments he'd made. "You're the ghost of—" he began, but his jaw felt like a block of wood.

> "What a wonderful highway! Well worth a wait of several hundred years."

The stranger swept into a low bow. "Appius Claudius, at your service. After all this time, I've finally seen my road. What a wonderful highway! Well worth a wait of several hundred years." He turned to the doorway. "By the way, I knew your ancestor, the first Calumnus. He was a good man. I considered him a friend."

And he vanished into the rain and fog outside.

Calumnus staggered onto a stool. His breathing was rapid, and his heart hammered in his chest. "It must have been a dream," he told himself. After all, ghosts didn't exist—did they? He must have drunk the wine himself and imagined the whole conversation. His breathing slowed. "Only a dream," he repeated again and again . . .

Until he glanced at the coin in his left hand. An old, old coin that looked like it had never been used. A coin that could have spent hundreds of years in a tomb. A coin minted during—

Calumnus swallowed hard.

During the days of Appius Claudius himself.

QUESTIONS TO CONSIDER

1. Why were roads important in the development of the Roman Empire?

2. How might it have been harder to construct a road in Roman times than today? How might it have been easier?

3. What other people from history can you think of who, like Appius Claudius, are mainly remembered today for one achievement?

Lucilla's Day

BY STEPHEN FEINSTEIN

Tuesday, 6th of Junius [June], 1:00 P.M.

I spent most of the morning at the baths, as usual. But I left the baths early, because today is a special day. This afternoon, I am hosting a banquet for Agrippina, the wife of Emperor Claudius. I admit I am not looking forward to this event. In fact, I am dreading it. But as the wife of Senator Vinicus, I am duty bound to honor that awful woman with a grand party. It's an important responsibility of a Roman **matron** to host banquets, and I have done so countless times for Vinicus's guests. Today,

---

People and Terms to Know

matron (MAY•truhn)—married woman who is mature in age and has high social standing.

Upper-class Roman women such as Lucilla often wore elaborate hair styles, which were created by their maidservants.

however, my husband is out of town on business. So I have invited only my women friends.

I hurried home through the hot streets of Rome, my servants rushing to keep up with me. My skin still tingled from my massage at the baths. It was not yet noon, and most people had not left for their midday rest. The streets were still crowded. Men made way for me at the sight of my long, flowing matron's dress. I ran into my friend, Helena, who asked me if I would be going to the theater today. I shook my head, smiled, and rushed on. When I passed one of the small shops that sells fine clothing, I went in. There I picked up the new **stola** that I had ordered specially for today's event. The long dress was just the right shade of purple, the color of royalty.

I was slightly out of breath by the time I arrived home. I crossed the sunny **atrium** and entered the cool rooms beyond. First I looked in on my children. They were taking their midday nap. Amalia, my

---

People and Terms to Know

stola (STOH•luh)—long, loose robe, with or without sleeves, worn by women in ancient Rome.

atrium (AY•tree•uhm)—main room of an ancient Roman house around which other rooms were built. It was open to the sky.

servant, said that their morning lessons with their tutor had gone well. "He was especially pleased at Cecilia's progress in arithmetic. Today she added all of her numerals correctly," Amalia reported.

I'm so proud of my dear little Cecilia. She's been reading since the age of five. Now that she is seven years old, I must begin teaching her how to spin, weave, and sew. These are just some of the skills a good Roman matron needs. Of course, her talent for numerals will allow her to help her future husband, whoever he may be, take care of family business matters.

"And what about my little Aulus (OW•luhs)?" I asked Amalia. "Has he learned the alphabet yet?"

"Well," she said, "mostly Aulus likes to play with his ivory letters. But today I saw him spell his name for the first time! The tutor says it's time for the boy to learn how to write letters. Next week, he will give Aulus a wax tablet and a **stylus**." You can imagine how pleased I was to hear that!

Next I made sure that my slaves had carried out all of my instructions about dinner. I tasted the various dishes, the special appetizers, and the main

---

People and Terms to Know

stylus (STY•luhs)—writing tool made from a pointed piece of wood, bone, or metal and shaped like a pencil.

courses. I began with the rose pie, made from calf's brains and roses fresh from my garden. It tasted fine, as did most of the other dishes. But there was something wrong with the parrot-tongue pie. It had not cooked properly and it didn't smell right.

"Silvanus," I shouted to our man who was removing bones from some fish. "Come over here and taste this!"

There was something wrong with the parrot-tongue pie.

Silvanus did as he was told. He frowned and forced himself to swallow the first bite. "I'm sorry, my lady. Something is wrong." The poor man looked very unhappy. I was annoyed. Of

▲
Lucilla might have used a case like this to hold her jewelry and makeup.

course, there will be quite enough to eat even without the parrot-tongue pie. I told Silvanus to give the pie to beggars in the street. Then I went to my rooms to rest for a while. When I finish writing this diary entry, I will take a short nap before getting dressed for dinner.

Tuesday, 6th of Junius [June], 9:00 P.M.

My guests began arriving at around three o'clock this afternoon. In walked my friends Portia, Iris, Galia, and several other wealthy Roman matrons. My servants led them to the three couches surrounding the low dining table. (I'm so glad I had the dining room walls decorated with scenes of guests at a banquet.) I joined my guests, dressed in my new purple stola and wearing my most elegant jewelry. The servants poured us drinks of that honeyed wine known as *mulsum*.

Agrippina arrived within the hour. I had hired horn players to welcome her. She made a grand entrance, and I saw her face flush with the special attention. There was a boy with Agrippina. I heard Galia whisper to Portia, "Look, she's brought her son Nero with her. They say that she dotes on Nero, spoiling him rotten."

Portia answered, "I'm sure that Agrippina lives for the day her Nero becomes emperor. It's clear she's been preparing him for that role."

The dinner entertainment I had arranged began with a pair of dancers. The two young women were accompanied by a drummer and flutist. Then a poet recited a long poem about the good qualities of the emperor Claudius. I noticed that Agrippina looked bored. Good heavens! I began to worry that I had failed to make a good impression. Then, Agrippina, who had been talking to Nero, looked up with a smile and clapped her hands. Nero stood up and walked to the middle of the room. He was carrying a **lyre**. Nero began to sing, accompanying himself on the lyre.

When Nero finished his first song, everyone clapped enthusiastically. He then began a second song. Agrippina couldn't take her eyes off him. She

---

People and Terms to Know

lyre (lyr)—stringed instrument somewhat like a small harp used by ancient peoples to accompany songs or the reciting of stories or poems.

is obviously very proud of him. A third song followed. And then a fourth. My guests clapped politely after each one. By the sixteenth song, Galia was having trouble keeping her eyes open. Perhaps it was the wine. She dozed briefly. If I had been sitting next to Galia, I would have poked her. When Galia opened her eyes, I noticed that Agrippina was staring at her—and she was not smiling. Galia also noticed.

Finally, the concert was over. Nero sat down again beside his mother. It was clear from the way he gazed at her that he adores her. Agrippina told us that she had hired a master musician from Greece, the home of the lyre, to come and give lessons to her "talented" son. And as if to prove that there was nothing she would not do for him, Agrippina added that her darling Nero was being tutored by none other than the great **Seneca**.

When the dinner party was over and my guests were leaving, I breathed a sigh of relief. It seemed that everything had gone well. Agrippina appeared to be

People and Terms to Know

Seneca (SEHN•uh•kuh)—(c. 4 B.C.–A.D. 65) Roman statesman, playwright, and philosopher.

in a jolly mood when she left. As Galia was leaving, she whispered to me, "Did you see the way Agrippina looked at me? That woman gives me chills!"

I told Galia, "I needn't remind you that for Roman matrons such as ourselves, tactfulness is as important as breathing! In our world—the world of senators, emperors, and empresses—a moment of carelessness could be dangerous, perhaps even fatal. So take care, my friend!"

Roman Numerals

Roman numerals are seldom used today. The Romans used letters to stand for numbers.
Here is the Roman system of writing numerals:

I = 1	C = 100
V = 5	D = 500
X = 10	M = 1,000
L = 50	

Fortunately, the world did not adopt the Roman system. Imagine having to subtract **CLV** from **M**! Instead, we use the familiar system of Arabic numerals that was developed in the Middle Ages.

QUESTIONS TO CONSIDER

1. What kind of life does Lucilla lead?
2. Why do you think Agrippina wanted her son to become emperor?
3. What does this story tell you about how people in the upper classes treated those they disliked or considered unimportant?
4. If you had been invited to Lucilla's dinner, what would you have thought about the food and entertainment?
5. How do you think Lucilla would have summed up the ideal Roman matron?

How Would You Survive as an Ancient Roman?
by Anita Ganeri

Anita Ganeri describes daily life in Rome in the first century A.D., including what Romans ate, what they wore, how they made a living, and what they did for entertainment.

The Roman Empire
by Martyn J. Whittock

Martyn J. Whittock uses a variety of materials to create a picture of the Roman Empire from its beginning to its fall. These materials include quotes from both ancient writers and later historians, works of art, and everyday objects.

The Ides of April
by Mary Ray

Mary Ray's historical novel presents Roman society from the point of view of a slave. In 62 A.D., a Roman senator is murdered. His slaves are imprisoned and face death unless the real murderer is found.

Buried Under Ten Feet of Ash

BY WALTER HAZEN

About 130 miles southeast of Rome lay the city of Pompeii. I say "lay," for it is no longer there. In the early afternoon hours of August 24 in the year 79, it was buried under volcanic ash when **Mount Vesuvius** erupted (exploded). Only the rooftops of houses were visible by the time the **pumice** and ashes settled.

My husband and I were lucky. We had left the city only hours before the disaster to return to our home in the country. Had we delayed our departure, we might not be alive today. Some 20,000 people

---

People and Terms to Know

Mount Vesuvius (vih•SOO•vee•uhs)—active volcano southeast of Naples, Italy. It is 4,000 feet high.
pumice (PUHM•ihs)—light, glassy, volcanic rock.

A street in Pompeii buried under ash when Mount Vesuvius (shown in the background) erupted in A.D. 79. Major digging to uncover the buried town did not occur until the 1800s. The stepping stones in the foreground enabled pedestrians to cross the street without getting wet.

lived in Pompeii. We were told that 2,000 of them died.

Before I write about Pompeii's final hours, let me tell you something about the city itself. It was a beautiful place with many gardens, fountains, and statues. It was also a favorite vacation spot for tourists. Its climate, shops, and amusements drew people from all over Italy. A large number of wealthy citizens even made their permanent homes there. Although small, the city constantly hummed with activity.

As with most of our cities, life in Pompeii centered around the forum. Here meetings were held and speeches were given. Here, too, were the shops that sold everything from bread to fruit to wine. Here also were the peddlers who sold their wares from little booths on the streets. By day, loud arguments between buyers and sellers filled the air. At night, the silence was broken by the cries of people going to and from the taverns.

I always enjoyed my trips into Pompeii to shop. I especially liked the raised sidewalks that kept one's feet dry when the streets were flooded. These sidewalks were very narrow, but they served the purpose. There were even large stepping stones where streets crossed. On these stones I could step over to the next sidewalk without getting wet.

Like many Roman towns, Pompeii had its amphitheater. More than 20,000 people filled its stands to watch gladiators fight to the death. I went there once, but I never returned. To my surprise, some of our women seem to enjoy these battles as much as the men do.

I have often wondered if some of the people killed when Vesuvius erupted were on their way to the amphitheater. Since gladiator fights were usually held in the afternoon, it is likely that they were. Some may have escaped, but I imagine most died a horrible death as pumice and ashes rained down on them.

As for my husband and myself, we were about halfway between Pompeii and Misenum, a town on the **Bay of Naples**, when the disaster occurred. The earth shook, and there was a loud explosion. The horse pulling our chariot panicked and nearly threw us to the ground. Turning, we saw that Vesuvius had blown its top. A great, black cloud was rising skyward. I could see columns of fire within the cloud. It wasn't long before the sky grew dark as night.

Poor Pompeii, I gasped! Right at the foot of the mountain, it was sure to be destroyed. All those people! And what about Herculaneum and Stabiae? Were these nearby towns to suffer the same fate? As events turned out, they were. Herculaneum was completely buried. Not even its rooftops were visible.

Hot ashes and rocks were soon falling all around us.

My husband decided that we should turn around and go back. He thought there were surely survivors who needed help. Although frightened, I favored going back too.

"Maybe there's nothing we can do, but I think we owe it to those poor people to try," he said.

He turned the chariot around and we struck out for Pompeii. We didn't get far. Hot ashes and rocks were soon falling all around us. As we neared the city, terrified people raced by with pillows tied to their heads. The pillows, we knew, were a desperate attempt to protect themselves from the burning rocks. Everyone we saw was shocked and dazed.

We stopped to comfort a little girl screaming for her mother. After some time, the mother appeared and stumbled off carrying the child in her arms. Other children were wandering around, crying for their parents. Husbands searched for wives and wives for husbands. Never have I witnessed such a scene. An old man passed us screaming that the end of the world had come.

We learned later that one of the victims was **Pliny the Elder**. In addition to being a naturalist and writer, Pliny was a government official. He was the commander of a group of ships anchored in the Bay of Naples. When he saw the smoke and fire coming from Vesuvius, he set sail for Pompeii. He never made it. While resting along the way, he died after breathing poisonous fumes from the volcano.

When it was safe to do so, people returned to Pompeii. They dug through the ashes and saved what they could of their valuables. They also carried away statues and other priceless objects.

People and Terms to Know

Pliny (PLIHN•ee) the Elder—(A.D. 23–79) Roman scholar who wrote a well-known book on natural history. His nephew, Pliny the Younger, described his uncle's death in his letters.

A plaster cast of a victim from Pompeii.

Will Pompeii rise again? Not likely. Although the people rebuilt their city after an earthquake in 62, this disaster is much worse. How is it possible to breathe life into a city that is buried under ten feet of ash?

QUESTIONS TO CONSIDER

1. What kinds of activities took place in the forum?
2. What prevented Pompeiians from getting out of the city safely?
3. What caused the death of Pliny the Elder?
4. How do we know about Pompeii today?
5. Why do you think people continue to live near active volcanoes such as Mount Vesuvius?

Pompeii: The Day a City Was Buried
by Melanie and Christopher Rice

On August 24 in A.D. 79, the Roman town of Pompeii was destroyed by a volcanic eruption of nearby Mount Vesuvius. The Rices recreate the world of Pompeii as it existed on that day.

A Roman Villa: The Inside Story
by Jacqueline Morley

Jacqueline Morley describes the life of a wealthy Roman family living on their villa in the countryside during the first century A.D.

Pompeii
by Peter Connolly

Peter Connolly presents a very detailed archaeological description of the ruins of Pompeii and a reconstruction of life in the ancient Roman city.

A Debate About the Roman Baths

BY MARIANNE McCOMB

My Dear Marcus,

Please excuse me if this letter interrupts your studies. I know the life of a student can be difficult, especially when exam time is near. But I feel I must say a bit more about the topic we discussed in front of the **Baths of Caracalla** today.

As you know, I am a great believer in **Epicureanism**. As such, I believe that pleasure is the highest good. I go to the baths to escape the worries of my daily life and embrace the more

---

People and Terms to Know

Baths of Caracalla (KAR•uh•KAL•uh)—public bath in Rome built by Caracalla, a Roman emperor from A.D. 211 to 217. Caracalla's was the largest public bath of its time and could hold around 1,600 bathers.

Epicureanism (EHP•ih•kyoo•REE•uh•NIHZ•uhm)—philosophy based on the principles of Epicurus, a Greek philosopher who taught that pleasure is the highest good. Epicureans also believed that true pleasure comes through self-control and that honorable behavior was important.

Around A.D. 65, the Romans began to build this public bath at Aquae Sulis (now Bath, England) in their province of Britannia.

pleasurable side of life. As I relax my weary body in the baths, I feel a wonderful peace of mind.

Of course, the baths allow for much more than just physical pleasure. As an Epicurean, I believe that the pleasures of the mind are far more important than those of the body. I cannot count how many times I've taken part in an interesting political or philosophical discussion while steaming away in the **calidarium**. Marcus, you of all people must see the value of lively discussion and debate!

As an Epicurean, I believe that the pleasures of the mind are far more important than those of the body.

Let me quote from the brilliant **Lucian**, who reveals himself here as an Epicurean. He makes clear what I have been struggling to say—

"On entering a bathhouse, one is received into a public hall of good size, with plenty of room for servants and attendants. On the left

People and Terms to Know

calidarium (KAL•ih•DAY•ree•uhm)—room in a public bath with heated pools.
Lucian (LOO•shun)—Greek writer of the 2nd century A.D. known for his wit.

are the lounging rooms, also of just the right sort for a bath, attractive, brightly lighted retreats. Then, beside them, a hall, larger than need be for the purposes of a bath, but necessary for the reception of richer persons. Next, large locker rooms to undress in, on each side, with a very high and brilliantly lighted hall between them, in which are three swimming pools of cold water. The hall is finished in **Laconian marble**, and has two statues of white marble in the ancient style, one of **Hygeia**, the other of **Aesculapius**.

"Then near this is another hall, the most beautiful in the world, in which one can stand or sit with comfort, linger without danger, and stroll about. Next comes the hot corridor. The hall beyond it is very beautiful, full of much light and aglow with color like that of purple hangings. It contains three hot tubs and is beautiful with other marks of thoughtfulness—with two toilets, many exits, and two devices for

People and Terms to Know

Laconian marble (luh•KOH•nee•uhn)—type of marble found in Greece.
Hygeia (hy•JEE•uh)—Greek goddess of health.
Aesculapius (EHS•kyuh•LAY•pee•uhs)—Roman god of medicine and healing.

telling time—a water clock that makes a bellowing sound, and a sundial."

Dear friend, please allow me to repeat my argument that the baths allow for both physical and intellectual pleasure. They refresh the body and the soul. Even you, Marcus, must agree with the benefits of that.

With fond regards, I remain your dear friend, Petronius

* * *

My Dear Friend Petronius,

I read with great interest your letter regarding the baths. I am pleased to continue our discussion of this topic. I find, however, that your letter has not convinced me to change my mind about these loud and dirty places. I must say that I see no beauty— or pleasure—in the baths, and consider them a terrible bother.

As I've mentioned to you before, you and your fellow Epicureans are doing a terrible wrong to

Rome. Epicureans spend their days searching for pleasure, while **Stoics** (like myself) keep the empire running smoothly. If it weren't for us, the work of this city would come to a grinding halt. Your claim that pleasure is the highest good is utterly ridiculous and terribly selfish. Petronius, it is goodness that is important. That along with hard work and civic duty. Life is meant to be taken seriously. How can a person be serious, hardworking, and dutiful if he is floating around in a deep pool?

In your letter, you mention that the baths are relaxing. Are they relaxing

> *Epicureans spend their days searching for pleasure, while Stoics (like myself) keep the empire running smoothly.*

for the slaves who must spend hour after hour tending the fierce fires that heat your calidarium? Are they relaxing for the poor men and women who come close to breaking their hands massaging the backs of the lazy citizens who lie upon their tables?

People and Terms to Know

Stoics—members of a school of philosophy known as Stoicism (STOH•ih•SIHZ•uhm). Stoics believed that virtue is the highest good and that wisdom, courage, justice, and temperance (moderation) were important human qualities. For the most part, Stoics were not interested in personal wealth or material possessions.

I must say, however, that your letter did inspire me in one way, my dear Petronius. I've spent an hour now reading and rereading this passage from the *Moral Letters*. These letters are some of Seneca's finest work. Please allow me to share this Stoic's viewpoint. It is most interesting. He says, in part:

"I live over a bathhouse. Imagine now the jarring mixture of noises. It makes you wish you were deaf! When the stronger fellows are exercising and swinging heavy leaden weights in their hands, when they are working hard or pretending to be working hard, I hear their groans. And whenever they release their pent-up breath, I hear their hissing and breathing. When I have to put up with a lazy fellow who is content with a cheap rubdown, I hear the slap of the hand pounding his shoulders. If now a professional ball player comes along and begins to keep score, I am done for. Add to this the arrest of a fighter or a thief, and the fellow who always likes to hear his own voice in the bath, and those who jump into the pool with a mighty splash as they strike the water. It disgusts me to list the varied cries of the sausage dealer and the one who sells sweets and of all the peddlers of the cook shop, hawking their wares, each with his own peculiar voice."

Dear friend, do not be surprised to hear me say that I will search for the meaning of life somewhere else than in the baths. Even you, Petronius, must accept that there's no reason why anyone should "refresh" the soul in a completely public place. So I must ask you: Why would I trade an hour of peaceful soul-searching and deep thinking for an hour of groaning, splashing, and shouting in a Roman bath? Indeed, why would anyone?

In all sincerity,
Marcus

QUESTIONS TO CONSIDER

1. What would you say Petronius and the Epicureans believed was most important in life?

2. What did Marcus and the Stoics believe was most important?

3. What are five characteristics of the Roman baths?

4. Which of the two letter writers—Marcus or Petronius—do you think makes the strongest argument? Support your answer.

Sources

Hannibal Dot Com *by Stephen Currie*

Benny, James, and Nico are fictional characters. The details in the story about Hannibal's army and the wars with Rome are historically accurate. Sources include *Hannibal: One Man Against Rome* by Harold Lamb (Garden City, NY: Doubleday & Company, Inc., 1958) and *Hannibal: Challenging Rome's Supremacy* by Sir Gavin de Beer (New York: Viking Press, 1969).

The Gracchi and the Roman Republic *by Judith Lloyd Yero*

Greek historians Plutarch and Appian have written about the lives of the Gracchi. Quotes about Caius's dream and his wife's pleas are from Plutarch. Historians are mixed in their opinions of the role of the Gracchi in the fall of the Roman Republic. For a collection of essays pro and con, see *Tiberius Gracchus: Destroyer or Reformer of the Republic?* by John M. Riddle (Lexington, MA.: D.C. Heath and Co., 1970).

Spartacus, Rebel Gladiator *by Marianne McComb*

Spartacus, Batiatus, and Crassus are historical figures. This story is a fictional account of real events. Spartacus's slave revolt was recorded by historians of his time who lived through it. *Spartacus and the Slave Wars* by Brent D. Shaw (New York: Bedford/St. Martins, 2000) includes translations of 80 original Greek and Latin documents on the daily life of slaves trained as gladiators and on the slave revolts.

Julius Caesar and His Friend Brutus *by Stephen Feinstein*
All the people in this story are real historical figures. The details of the story, including the warning from the sooth-sayer, come to us from *Parallel Lives* by the Roman historian Plutarch, who wrote his portrait of Julius Caesar in A.D. 75, a little more than one hundred years after Caesar's death. William Shakespeare made this story famous by writing a play about it. More information about Julius Caesar can be found in *When the World Was Rome: 753 B.C. to A.D. 476* by Polly Schoyer Brooks and Nancy Zinsser Walworth (Philadelphia; New York: J. B. Lippincott Company, 1972).

Cleopatra, Egypt's Last Pharaoh *by Barbara Littman*
The characters in this story are all real historical figures, and the events are based on historical accounts. There are many sources of information about Cleopatra. Among them are *Cleopatra: The Story of a Queen* by Emil Ludwig (New York: Viking Press, 1937).

Caesar Augustus *by Walter Hazen*
Favius, the narrator, is a fictional character. Julius Caesar, Octavian (who becomes Caesar Augustus), Mark Antony, Marcus Lepidus, Cleopatra, Octavia, Virgil, and Horace are all real historical figures. This period in history was well documented both in writings of the time and in the works of later historians. A good source is *What Life Was Like When Rome Ruled the World 100 B.C.–A.D. 200* by the editors of Time-Life Books (Alexandria, VA: Time-Life Books, 1997).

Who Killed Claudius? *by Judith Lloyd Yero*

All the characters in this story are real historical figures. More details about the Emperor Claudius and his nasty family can be found in *Chronicle of the Roman Emperors: The Reign-by-Reign Record of the Rulers of Imperial Rome* by Christopher Scarre (Thames & Hudson; distributed by W. W. Norton, New York, 1995).

Paul Spreads Christianity *by Lynnette Brent*

The Roman centurion who narrates this story is fictional. Paul and the emperor Nero are historical figures. The details of the setting in this story are based on records from the time. Paul's journey and difficulties are well-documented. One source for this story is the book of Acts in the Bible. Paul's life is also detailed in *History of the World* by J. M. Roberts (New York: Oxford University Press, 1993).

A Soldier's Life *by Stephen Feinstein*

Quintus is a fictional character. The details about the life of a Roman soldier during the war with Parthia are historically accurate. Sources include *Roman Life* by Mary Johnston (Glenview, IL: Scott, Foresman, 1957) and *A History of Rome: Selections* by Livy, translated and with an introduction by Moses Hadas and Joe P. Poe (New York: Modern Library, 1962).

The Appian Way *by Stephen Currie*

The ghost of Appius Claudius and the innkeeper Calumnus are fictional, as is their story. Appius Claudius really lived. The sources for this story include *Roman Roads* by Raymond Chevallier, Translated by N.H. Field (Berkeley and Los Angeles, CA: University of California Press, 1976); *Roman Roads* by Victor W. Von Hagen (Cleveland and New York: The World Publishing Company, 1966); and *Merchants, Pilgrims and Highwaymen: A History of Roads Through the Ages* by Hermann Schreiber (New York: G. P. Putnam's Sons, 1961).

Lucilla's Day *by Stephen Feinstein*

Lucilla and her friends are fictional characters and Lucilla's journal is fiction. Agrippina and her son Nero are historical figures. Seneca also really lived. The information about a day in the life of a Roman senator's wife is historically factual. You can read more about daily life in ancient Rome in *Ancient Rome* by Mike Corbishley (New York: Facts On File, 1981) and in *Ancient Rome* by Judith Simpson, Paul Roberts, consulting editor (Alexandria, VA: Time-Life Books, 1997).

Buried Under Ten Feet of Ash *by Walter Hazen*

The narrator and her husband are fictional characters. Pliny the Elder is an historical figure. We know about the destruction of Pompeii on August 24, A.D. 79, both from the writings of people who lived through it as well as from the work of archaeologists who have uncovered the city. A good source is *Caesar and Christ* by historian Will Durant (New York: Simon and Schuster, 1944).

A Debate About the Roman Baths *by Marianne McComb*

Marcus and Petronius are fictional characters. The philosophers they quote, Lucian and Seneca, are real historical figures. The quotes are from translations of their writings. The descriptions of their world, including the baths, is based on ancient documents. You can read about them in *The Ancient Romans* by Chester Starr (Oxford: Oxford University Press, 1971).

Glossary of People and Terms to Know

Actium (AK•shee•uhm)—piece of land that juts out into the Ionian Sea off the west coast of Greece.

Aeneid (ih•NEE•ihd)—Virgil's long poem about the hero Aeneas. Romulus and Remus, legendary twins of early Rome, were said to be Aeneas's grandsons.

Aesculapius (es•kyuh•LAY•pee•us)—Roman god of medicine and healing.

Agrippina (AG•ruh•PYN•uh) **the Younger**—(c. A.D. 15–59) Roman empress, fourth wife of Cladius and mother of the emperor Nero.

amphitheaters (AM•fuh•THEE•uh•tuhrs)—circular or oval buildings used as sports arenas. Some were large enough to hold 50,000 people.

Antony, Mark (AN•tuh•nee)— (82–30 B.C.) Roman general and statesman; a friend of Caesar.

Appian (AP•ee•uhn) **Way**—first major road in Roman territory. When the original construction was finished in the third century B.C., the road ran from Rome south to the town of Capua. Later it was extended to the town of Brindisi, further south. Some parts of the Appian Way are still in use today.

Appius Claudius—man who directed the beginning of construction on the Appian Way in the fourth century B.C.

aqueduct (AK•wih•DUHKT)— channel used to carry water from the mountains to the cities and surrounding farmlands.

assassinated—murdered by surprise attack, usually for political reasons. The murder itself is called an *assassination*.

atrium (AY•tree•uhm)—main room of an ancient Roman house around which other rooms were built. It was open to the sky.

Augustus—see **Imperator Augustus**.

barbarians (bahr•BAIR•ee•uhns)— people who lived beyond the borders of the Roman Empire and were considered by the Romans to be uncivilized.

Baths of Caracalla (KAR•uh•KAL•uh)—public bath in Rome built by Caracalla, a Roman emperor from A.D. 211 to 217.

Bay of Naples (NAY•puhlz)—bay in southwest Italy.

Brutus—(85–42 B.C.) appointed governor of a Roman province in northern Italy by Caesar after the defeat of Pompey.

Caesar, Julius (JOOL•yuhs SEE•zuhr)—(100–44 B.C.) Roman general, statesman, and historian.

Caesarea (SEE•zuh•REE•uh)— ancient Roman capital of Judea (now Israel). Judea was part of the Roman Empire.

calidarium (KAL•ih•DAY•ree•uhm)—room in a bathhouse with heated pools.

Caligula (kuh•LIHG•yuh•luh)— emperor of Rome (A.D. 37–41). He was a ruthless, wasteful leader. He once made his soldiers fill their helmets with seashells, declaring himself victor over the gods of the sea.

Cannae (KAN•ee)—village in southeastern Italy, where Hannibal defeated the Romans in 216 B.C. About 50,000 Romans were killed, compared to about 6,000 soldiers in Hannibal's army.

cape—piece of land jutting out into the water.

Capua (CAP•yoo•uh)—town south of Rome and a wealthy farming community.

Cassius (KASH•uhs)—(d. 42 B.C.) Roman general and leader of the plot against Caesar.

centurions (sehn•TUR•ee•uhns)— Roman army officers who commanded companies of 100 men.

Claudius (KLAW•dee•uhs)— (10 B.C.–A.D. 54) ruler of the Roman Empire from A.D. 41 to 54, Claudius succeeded to the throne after the assassination of Caligula.

Cleopatra (KLEE•uh•PAT•ruh)— (c. 69–30 B.C.) queen of ancient Egypt from 47 to 30 B.C.

Crassus, Marcus Licinius— (c. 115–53 B.C.) charming, greedy, and powerful Roman leader. At one time, the richest man in Rome.

crucified (kru•suh•FYD)—put to death by being hung upon a large wood cross until the lungs were crushed by the weight of the body. Death was by suffocation.

Cydnus River (SIHD•nuhs)— river that ran into the Turkish city of Tarsus.

Dacians (DAY•shuns)—inhabitants of Dacia.

Epicureanism (EHP•ih•kyoo•REE•uh•NIHZ•uhm)— philosophy based on the principles of Epicurus, a Greek philosopher who taught that pleasure is the highest good. Epicureans also believed that self-control and honorable behavior were important.

"Et tu, Brute?"—the Latin words *et tu* mean "and you," but Caesar's last words are usually translated as "You too, Brutus?"

forum—marketplace or public place in ancient Rome, in which courts of law and public business was conducted.

Gaul—ancient country of western Europe in the region occupied by present-day France.

gladiator (GLAD•ee•AY•tuhr)— slave or paid fighter trained to fight other fighters or wild animals as public entertainment.

Gracchus, Gaius (GY•uhs GRAK•uhs)—(153–121 B.C.) Younger son of Tiberius Gracchus and Cornelia. Gaius was a more fiery speaker than his older brother.

Gracchus, Tiberius (ty•BEER•ee•uhs GRAK•uhs)— (163–133 B.C.) Elder son of Tiberius Gracchus, a Roman consul and Cornelia, daughter of Scipio Africanus, the conqueror of Hannibal. Tiberius was known as a brave soldier and a calm, but powerful, speaker.

granaries (GRAN•uh•reez)— buildings for storing grain.

Hannibal (HAN•uh•buhl)— (247–183 B.C.) general from Carthage, a city-state on the Mediterranean coast of Africa. Hannibal was Rome's enemy in the Second Punic War.

Horace—Roman poet of the first century B.C. Among his writings was a description of a trip he made along the Appian Way.

Hygeia (hy•JEE•uh)—Greek goddess of health.

Imperator Augustus (IHM•puh•RAH•tawr aw•GUHS•tuhs)—first Roman emperor. He ruled from 27 B.C. to A.D. 14. The word *imperator* meant "conqueror." In time, it evolved into *emperor*.

Jerusalem (juh•ROO•suh•luhm)— ancient city in Judea that had been the capital of the Jewish kingdom, conquered by the Romans.

Jews—descendants of the ancient Israelites. Judaism was a major religion throughout the Roman Empire.

Laconian marble (luh•KONE•ee•un)—type of marble found in Greece.

legion (LEE•jun)—company of 3,000 to 6,000 foot soldiers and 300 to 700 men on horseback.

Lucian (LOO•shun)—Greek writer of the 2nd century A.D. known for his wit.

lyre (lyr)—stringed instrument somewhat like a small harp used by ancient peoples to accompany songs or the reciting of stories or poems.

matron (MAY•trun)—married woman who is mature in age and has high social standing.

Messalina, Valeria (vuh•LEER•ee•uh MEHS•uh•LYN•uh) —third wife of Claudius. She and Claudius had two children.

Mount Vesuvius (vih•SOO•vee•uhs)—active volcano southeast of Naples, Italy. It is 4,000 feet high.

Nero (NEER•oh)—(A.D. 37–68) Emperor of Rome A.D. 54–68. He may have set the great fire of Rome in 64.

Octavian (ahk•TAY•vee•uhn)— (63 B.C.–14 A.D.) one of three members of a triumvirate who ruled Rome. He later had the title of Augustus.

Parthia (PAHR•thee•uh)— ancient country in Asia, now in northeast Iran.

Parthians—inhabitants of the Parthian Empire (ancient Persia) in what is now Iran.

Paul—Roman citizen and a Jew who was an early convert to Christianity. He established Christian churches in many countries and wrote most of the letters in the New Testament of the Bible. He was born in Tarsus and died about A.D. 67.

pharaoh (FAIR•oh)—any of the rulers of ancient Egypt.

plebeians (plih•BEE•uhns)— common people of ancient Rome.

Pliny (PLIHN•ee) the Elder— (A.D. 23–79) Roman scholar who wrote a well-known book on natural history.

Pompey (PAHM•pee)—(106–48 B.C.) Roman general and statesman.

Praetorian Guard (pree•TAWR•ee•uhn)—soldiers who guarded the life of the emperor; bodyguards.

pumice (PUHM•ihs)—light, glassy, volcanic rock.

reign (RAYN)—years a ruler is in power.

Roman Senate—group of officials who helped govern Rome.

Scipio Africanus (SIHP•ee•oh af•rih•KAHN•us)—(c. 237–183 B.C.) great Roman general who won the Battle of Zama. He let Hannibal return to Carthage, but made Carthage become a Roman ally.

Seneca (SEN•uh•kuh)— (4 B.C.–A.D. 65) Roman statesman, playwright, and philosopher.

Spartacus (SPAHR•tuh•kuhs)— gladiator from Thrace, a country on the Black Sea. He led a slave revolt in 73–71 B.C.

stadia—plural of *stadium*, Roman unit of distance equal to about 600 feet.

Stoics—members of a school of philosophy known as stoicism. Stoics believed that virtue is the highest good and that wisdom, courage, justice, and temperance (moderation) were important human qualities.

stola (STOH•luh)—long, loose robe, with or without sleeves, worn by women in ancient Rome.

stylus (STY•lus)—writing tool made from a pointed piece of wood, bone, or metal shaped like a pencil.

toga (TOH•guh)—loose outer garment worn in public by citizens of ancient Rome.

Trajan—(A.D. 53–117) Roman emperor, A.D. 98–117.

tribune—representative, elected by the people's assembly. There were ten tribunes, any one of whom could call the people's assembly together or forbid that a proposal come before the assembly.

triumvirate (try•UHM•vuhr•iht)—ruling body of three people.

veto—in Latin, the word means "I deny." If a tribune vetoed a law, it could not come before the people for a vote. Today, the word is used somewhat differently. A president can veto a law presented by Congress, but Congress can still pass the law if two thirds of the members vote for it.

Zama (ZAY•muh)—North African site of the final battle in the Second Punic War (202 B.C.). Rome won; Carthage lost.

Acknowledgements

9 © North Wind Picture Archives.
10, 15 © The Granger Collection.
17 Photograph by Erich Lessing/
Art Resource.
20 © The Granger Collection.
22 Scala/Art Resource, NY.
27 © The Granger Collection.
38 © Art Resource, NY.
45 Giraudon/Art Resource, NY.
49 © Archivo Iconografico, S.A./
Corbis.
55 © Scala/Art Resource, NY.
56 © Archivo Iconografico, S.A./
Corbis.
58 SuperStock International.
66 © North Wind Picture Archives.
68 © Archivo Iconografico/Corbis.
77 © Hulton Getty Picture
Collection.
78 © Archivo Iconografico/Corbis.
81 © The Granger Collection.

86, 88 Alinari/Art Resource, NY.
90 © Hulton Getty Picture
Collection.
94 SEF/Art Resource, NY.
99 © The Granger Collection.
106 © The Granger Collection.
111 © SuperStock International.
114 © The Granger Collection.
117 © Hulton Getty Picture
Collection.
126 © Fox Photos.
129 © The Granger Collection.
135 © Hulton Getty Picture
Collection.
137 © Photograph by Erich
Lessing/Art Resource, NY.
142 © The Granger Collection.
143 © Photograph by Erich
Lessing/Art Resource, NY.
145 © Hulton Getty Picture Library.